Shaadi Remix

D1521946

Shaadi Remix

Transforming the Traditional Indian Marriage

GEETHA RAVINDRA

Shaadi Remix: Transforming the Traditional Indian Marriage

Published by Wheatmark®
1760 East River Road, Suite 145
Tucson, Arizona 85718 U.S.A.
www.wheatmark.com

ISBN: 978-1-60494-948-3 (paperback)
ISBN: 978-1-60494-968-1 (ebook)
LCCN: 2013934246

rev201301

I DEDICATE THIS BOOK TO MY DEAR HUSBAND RAVI, MY SOUL mate and best friend, who has always supported me in all my endeavors and who showed me that love after marriage really is possible; to my amazing children Lakshmi and Krishna, who bring me immeasurable happiness and meaning in my life, and who balance the Indian and American cultures beautifully; and to my wonderful parents M.B. and Shantha Veerabhadrappa, who gave me the spiritual foundation and values that continue to guide me.

Disclaimer: The cases described in this book are from real life experiences, but the names and details have been changed. Readers may identify with certain situations described in the book. However, each couple's situation described in the book reflects an amalgamation of the stories of dozens of couples I have had the honor of working with. I am a humble devotee of the Hindu faith. I intend no disrespect to either Hinduism or Indian marriage cultural traditions in writing this book. I also do not hold myself out to be an expert on the Vedic scriptures and ask forgiveness for any mistakes I may have unknowingly made in the religious references or interpretations noted in the book. Hari Om.

Contents

Preface

SHAADI, OR MARRIAGE, IS THE MOST SACRED INSTITUTION in India. The marriage ceremony is the thirteenth ceremony among sixteen ceremonies in a Hindu's life. It is a holy sacrament solemnized in accordance with rituals enjoined in the Vedas, the ancient scriptures of Hinduism. In Indian families, from the moment a baby girl is born, parents begin saving and planning for that momentous occasion when they will give their precious child to her husband to love and to cherish. Vedic scriptures describe the wedding ceremony literally as the gifting of a young maiden from her father to her future husband, or *Kanyadaana*. When Indian parents successfully get their children married, it is considered a huge accomplishment, and they feel tremendous joy and relief from fulfilling one of life's most important responsibilities.

For centuries, marriage between Indians has been a commitment for life. The concept of divorce is still taboo to the vast majority of the Indian population. If a husband and wife don't get along, the wife is expected to adjust and make things work. Some amount of flexibility is expected in any new relationship, yet in Indian society this burden falls primarily on the wife. Women are instructed by their mothers, sisters, aunts, and grandmothers to concede to their husband's wishes and expectations, with the hope that they will be able to win their husband's heart and ultimately lead a happy life together.

Preface

The Hindu belief in karma and dharma also impacts traditional perspectives on marriage. Karma, the belief that everything happens as a consequence of past deeds, is integral to the Hindu faith. If a woman or man has an unhappy marriage, the community assumes it is because of some bad actions they committed in a previous life. There is also an important Hindu belief that one must do his duty, or dharma. Dharma requires men and women to marry, as that is an integral part of being a *householder*, which is a key stage in life. The Vedas divide human life into four stages, *brahmacharya ashrama* (student), *grahastha ashrama* (householder), *vanaprastha ashrama* (retirement), and *sannyasa ashrama* (renunciation). Dharma forces one to remain married, even if it is an unhappy or difficult relationship, in order to fulfill responsibilities to family and to society during the grahastha stage.

Another very important cultural factor for many Indians is saving face. An Indian's reputation is a critical part of her identity and self-respect. Being divorced in Indian society carries with it a strong stigma. Couples often prefer to remain in an unhappy marriage in order to protect their image as an ideal Indian family, regardless of the pain and heartache the marriage may bring each day. When an Indian marriage fails, there is often a tremendous sense of guilt, shame, and fear of social rebuke. As a result, couples strive to remain together, no matter how painful the situation, in an effort to protect their reputation and children from the challenges associated with divorce, and to save face in the community.

Although India can proudly declare that nearly 100 percent of its marriages are a success, recent urbanization and women's growing financial independence are causing the divorce rate to rise. Gender equality is now giving rise to ego clashes between the husband and wife, especially if the wife is also well educated and employed. The empowerment of women has stimulated the dissolution of marriage in urban areas in India and among Indians around the world. Indian women are now open to the option of ending their marital relationship, as opposed to silently bearing lifelong abuses, as generations of women did before them.

As an attorney and mediator of Indian origin, over the past twenty years I have assisted hundreds of divorcing or separating American families in resolving issues related to contested custody, visitation, and support matters. I have also helped numerous men and women of Indian origin deal with issues of marital discord, domestic violence, adultery, alcoholism, and desertion. Because the idea of divorce in Indian marriages is no longer as unimaginable as it once was and the number of divorces is steadily rising, I am concerned about the future of the sacred institution of marriage in the Indian community. The commitment to India's system of marriage is waning among the younger generation. The paradigm of the traditional Hindu marriage and the premises upon which it is based do not translate logically or easily in the twenty-first century. The viability of the Indian marriage and the family unit is dependent upon younger generations of Indians better understanding the purpose of Hindu marriage traditions, thoughtfully considering which customs and values they wish to retain, and determining how they choose to honor and preserve the sanctity of marriage in the modern era.

The purpose of this book is to provide an overview of the factors Indian families have traditionally relied upon in arranging Hindu marriages, and to highlight that primary consideration of these criteria today may no longer lead to successful marriages. Contemporary approaches to identifying a compatible partner that blend a commitment to the Hindu values of trust, respect, love, and friendship, as well as good communication and effective conflict resolution skills, are examined to provide a more practical approach for younger generations to enjoy a successful marriage.

Shaadi Remix

Introduction

T HE TRADITIONAL VEDIC MARRIAGE IS AN INSTITUTION that is as old, strong, and solid as a glacier. The source of the Hindu marriage ceremony is the *Rig Veda*, which is described by scholars as the oldest book in the world. A Hindu marriage joins two individuals for life so that they can pursue dharma (duty), *artha* (wealth), *kama* (physical desires), and *moksha* (ultimate spiritual salvation) together.

The traditional Vedic marriage is, much like the world's glaciers, undergoing a slow but steady transformation. Over the course of the past few decades, this beautiful fortress of Indian society has been gradually eroding as a result of significant socioeconomic changes in India, increased mobility of Indians, greater gender equality in Indian education, and the Westernization of Indians at home and abroad.

To illustrate some of the changes to the Indian marriage, the stories on the following pages are examples of the challenges many Indian marriages currently face.

Couple 1

Kalpana and her family moved to the United States when she was four years old. She grew up enjoying her comfortable and independent lifestyle in America and connected especially strongly with America's music, clothes, and food. After graduating from college, Kalpana had an arranged marriage with Ram, a young man from her regional community in India. Kalpana met Ram during a brief visit to India with her parents, and they were married within weeks of their introduction. Ram arrived in the United States a few months later but did not like it. He missed his family, felt like a fish out of water, and insisted to Kalpana that they move back to India. Kalpana was frustrated by his unwillingness to try to adjust to America, saddened by her failing marriage, and confused about what she should do next. She refused to give up her lifestyle, friends, and family for her new husband, whom she barely knew. She worried about breaking her family's hearts if she told them about her problems with Ram. They had spent a great deal on her wedding and were finally at peace, having completed the marriage of their last daughter.

Couple 2

Meera grew up in the United States. She married Jagan after his family assisted her family in India during a time of great need. Jagan joined Meera in the United States soon after they got married. Meera's sister and her brother-in-law, who were like parents to her, live near her. She enjoyed their company and spent a great deal of time with them. Jagan did not like his sister-in-law and believed she interfered in their family affairs. He left Meera to visit a distant relative in another state, and then refused to move back in with Meera. He told her to move in with him and his relatives. Meera struggled with whether to quit her job and move to another state with Jagan, as he suggested. She was worried about their complete lack of communication so early on in their marriage. She wished Jagan would respect her sister and her need for familial support. She was concerned that Jagan was not comfortable relying on her income, and yet she did not see him making an effort to find a job. Meera was worried about the negative image reflected on her family if she elected to get divorced. She was still young and wondered whether anyone would marry her in the future if she were to get a divorce.

Couple 3

Deepak married Sonia in India, and the two of them returned to his home in the United States after the wedding. Sonia was homesick, and she invited her parents to visit her in the United States. They were surprised at how small Deepak's apartment was and could not believe that their daughter was expected to cook and clean. They offered Deepak a high-paying job and big home in India if he would move back. Deepak liked the United States and worked hard for what he had. He did not want to live off of his in-laws and refused the offer. Sonia was disappointed, and after one particularly loud and difficult argument in which she was shoved against a door, she called the police to report domestic violence. The judge prohibited Deepak from coming into their home or near his wife until their next court hearing and issued an emergency protective order. Deepak loved Sonia but did not feel that he could trust her anymore. He wished that his in-laws would stop interfering in their marriage, but he did not know whether that would ever happen. He had the option of marrying any number of young women in India but chose Sonia because of her family's background and status. He now feared that her expectations of a luxurious lifestyle would never be satisfied in the United States.

Couple 4

Maya had a boyfriend whom she loved and planned on living with the rest of her life. Her boyfriend, however, married another woman at the insistence of his family. In an effort to assist Maya in getting out of the slump this heartbreak had caused, her cousin introduced her to his close friend Anil. Anil had been introduced to several women by his parents, but no one was to his liking. When he met Maya, he found her attractive and was open to the idea of marriage. Maya's father liked Anil and was worried about his daughter's future. She was not getting any younger, and she would not be marketable if people knew about her previous relationship. Maya's father convinced her to marry Anil.

The couple's honeymoon period lasted exactly that long—the duration of the honeymoon. Maya quickly began to find fault in Anil's personality. She wanted him to be more outgoing and competitive. She wanted him to leave India and develop a thriving business. She enjoyed an active social life and expected to go out to dinner every night. She disliked Anil's family immensely, finding them to be uncultured and beneath her family's status. She demanded that Anil buy a separate home for them in one of the most expensive districts in the city. Anil bent over backwards to try to please Maya, but he was unsuccessful. He held out hope that Maya would change, or that she would accept him for who he was. Maya blamed her father for forcing her to marry Anil.

The marriages in all these examples unfortunately ended in divorce. Three of these couples involve Indians who live in the United States and went back to India to get married, and one example is that of a couple that resides in India. Regardless of where they grew up or where they live, all these couples have in common their traditional Indian cultural upbringing and the Hindu faith. Yet, unlike hundreds of thousands of Indian marriages that have succeeded in the past, these more recent marriages did not. Why is it that Indian marriages have worked for centuries, but now so many struggle to survive? In working with dozens of Indian couples seeking a divorce, I have been contemplating these issues not only as a professional mediator and attorney but also as a second-generation Indian woman who was raised in the United States, got married through the arranged marriage system, and has been happily married for over twenty years. To better understand the lens through which I consider the subject of the traditional Indian marriage and its future, a brief overview of my personal life and background is useful.

I was born to Indian immigrants from the state of Karnataka who moved to the United States in 1970 seeking a better standard of living. This was a period in US history when the immigration laws were loosened up, permitting a major influx of professionals from Asia. My father, a young engineer, took advantage of this opportunity and moved to the United States seeking better job opportunities and a higher standard of living. I was among the earliest second-generation Indians in the United States and was raised according to the very strict cultural expectations of my parents, who grew up in India in the 1950s.

To better understand the mindset of my parents as they raised me, a snapshot of the India of my parents' generation, and in particular of my mother's upbringing, is helpful. My maternal grandparents had six children. My mother was the second oldest.

Introduction

She was prohibited from attending college, although she wanted to study further. She was never allowed to step outside the house, much less watch passersby from the front portico. As a young girl, she recalled that once a neighbor's child went missing at a town fair, and she was asked by the child's mother to assist in looking for the child. She searched for this child, along with the neighbor and a few other children. The child was ultimately found, and my mother returned home. Upon reaching home she was beaten severely by her father, my grandfather, for wandering around the neighborhood without parental supervision. Her father was not afraid for her safety but afraid of what others would think about the freedom her parents gave her to walk on the road unattended. That experience has remained embedded in my mother's mind even to this day. As a young woman, she never spoke to any man, not even her cousins or uncles. She never saw or spoke to my father before the day of her marriage. Even after marriage, my mother was afraid to go to a movie or dinner with my father for fear that her father would scold or punish her for accompanying a man in public. So, while the traditions, values, and culture had been evolving in India throughout the 1970s and 1980s, my world at home in America remained stagnant in the India of the 1960s, as that was the frame of reference my parents carried with them when they moved to the United States.

As a teenager, I visited India in the 1980s during summer holidays and was stunned at the girls who cut their hair short and wore pants. I, on the other hand, was not permitted to cut my hair, which had grown past my waist, and I was allowed to wear only long skirts or Indian clothes during these visits. It seemed as though I had to work even harder than my peers in India to prove I was Indian. I learned classical Carnatic music, visited numerous temples, performed several special pujas (prayers), and studied Hinduism.

As a teenager, I participated in the arranged marriages of two

9

uncles. Along with my mother, I accompanied my uncles on brief trips to India. I know that my mother was required for these important visits, as my paternal grandfather died when I was very young and my uncles looked upon my parents as their own parents. I believe that I was also brought along on these trips to observe the arranged marriage system that I would soon be expected to follow.

Working with a marriage broker, we visited the homes of several young women who served us tea, milk, and sweets as the families considered the potential match. I quietly marveled as my uncles considered the suitability of each woman and was amazed at how quickly marriages could be arranged. From start to finish this process took only weeks.

Growing up, there was an implied expectation that I too would one day have an arranged marriage. I was prohibited from dating or even having boys as friends. My father was very protective, and I recall being one of only a handful of students precluded from attending sex education in middle-school health class. As a teenager, these limitations had a negative impact on my self-confidence and ability to feel a part of my peer group. I grew up feeling tremendous pressure to be successful academically, but I could have no part in school socially. I was not permitted to attend school dances or even participate in school sports, as that could involve interaction with boys. As I grew older, I overcame my feelings of insecurity and fortunately had many Indian friends with similar limitations, as well as American friends who respected my cultural differences. I also had a very loving and positive relationship with my parents, despite these restrictions.

I understood very early on that I had to marry a boy of my parent's choosing or risk bringing shame to my family and being disowned. Knowing that I was going to have an arranged marriage, I decided to at least control the timing of my marriage.

Introduction

I chose to get married upon the completion of my first year in law school. I reasoned that any man I married would need at least a year or two to get settled professionally, and that would coincide with my completion of law school. I could then make an informed decision as to job opportunities. While I clearly was not in control of the method of marriage, I felt a tremendous need to control and plan other aspects of my life.

I went to India at the conclusion of my first-year exams. My father had carefully preselected a few eligible bachelors that family members had recommended. I was asked to serve tea and snacks to the young men and their families, who visited my uncle's home in Bangalore. I barely saw the men who came to see me and often felt like a show horse being paraded around for public scrutiny and appraisal. The young man who is now my husband of over twenty years was my father's favorite because he believed we had several common interests, including our love of debate and drama. I spoke privately with my husband for approximately ten minutes. I do not recall the details of what we discussed, just that he was the only man I had met in India who asked me what my interests were and did not spend the entire conversation glorifying his own achievements. It was after the engagement that I really got to know my husband and, fortunately, grew to love him.

In short, my entire upbringing revolved around my marriage. My parents worked tirelessly to keep me in a secure Indian cultural bubble while living in the United States. My teenage hormones were suppressed; my opportunities to meet or talk to boys, much less fall in love, were nonexistent; I performed special pujas to Lord Shiva as a teenager to ensure I was blessed with a good husband; the goal that was drilled into my head was to marry a good boy that my parents selected and to lead a happy family life. I did not contest my parents' expectations out of sheer respect and love for them. I knew that it would break their hearts if I were to challenge them or refuse to marry according to the traditional Indian customs. Intellectually, I had observed enough Indian marriages to note that most of them seemed to work, regardless of the fact they were arranged. I put my complete trust and confidence in my parents' selection of an appropriate partner for me, knowing that they would want only the best for me. Likewise, my husband, who was raised in India, was also committed to the arranged marriage process and trusted his parents in the selection of an appropriate bride. He too had not had any prior relationships with women and was saving his heart for the one he would marry.

After twenty-two years of marriage, I can sincerely say that I could not have found such an incredibly wonderful man as my husband if I had searched to the ends of the earth. On the other hand, as the mother of a teenage daughter and son, I could never imagine suggesting that they marry someone I chose after having met for ten minutes, as I was expected to. Similarly, it is highly unlikely that most Indian children raised in the United States or abroad today would have the same trust and confidence in the arranged marriage system.

So what has changed? Why did I place my trust and confidence in the arranged marriage system for my own marriage but now protest its application in the lives of my children? The answer is closely related to my observations about why Indian arranged marriages are increasingly breaking down. The primary reason I believe Indian marriages are failing today is because many of the traditional premises upon which arranged marriages are based no longer serve a meaningful purpose. Also, the shared commitment to the concept and ideals of an arranged marriage, which requires enormous trust in the judgment of parents and was an intrinsically valued social norm inculcated in young people in India in decades past, is less honored today. It has been replaced by the strong, overwhelming desire among young adults for autonomy and self-determination.

Today, there are fewer arranged marriages among the wealthy and well educated, especially among those who have moved out of India. In recent years, the number of Indian marriages resulting in divorce has grown. Unfortunately, it is difficult to find current statistics on divorce in India. Recent news stories and Internet articles provide some data. One survey suggests that in the 1960s, there were only one to two divorces per year in Delhi. This number grew to one to two hundred divorces in the 1980s. In the 1990s this number expanded to one thousand divorce cases a year. In this decade, the number of divorces in Delhi has grown to approximately nine thousand cases a year. In the 1980s Delhi had two courts to handle divorce matters; today it has sixteen. In 2006 in Bangalore, the IT hub of India, it was recorded that 1,246 cases of divorce were filed. It has been estimated Mumbai shot up to seven thousand cases in 2007, while cities that are acknowledged for their cultural richness and social values, like Kolkata and Chennai, are not far behind. States like Punjab and Haryana are now seeing an increase of 150 percent in the divorce rate over the last decade. Kerala, known to be the most literate state, has experienced an increase of divorce rate by 350 percent in the last ten years. Individuals between the ages of twenty-five and thirty-five filed 70 percent of the divorce cases. Eighty-five percent of the marriages ended in divorce in the first three years of marriage.

These statistics require older and younger Indians to stop and reflect on whether the traditional arranged marriage model that dictated how Hindu marriages are made is out of sync with modern society. There is greater societal acceptance of divorcees in urban areas in India and abroad. Parents have come to recognize that their daughter can have a life after marriage without a husband, particularly if she is well educated. The anonymity of big cities has helped divorced people avoid the glare of judgmental friends, relatives, and society. Indians are increasingly mobile in India and around the world and have fewer connections with a specific Indian community. Women enjoy financial freedom to walk away from an unhealthy relationship. They no longer have to rely on their husband for everything.

Changing gender roles are a source of marital conflict Many women have good jobs or at least an education with which to get a job. Traditionally women were expected to care for the home and children. Now, as women are pursuing careers, they are under more stress and seek a spousal partnership in which the man will share responsibilities at home. Some men are uncomfortable with an independent working spouse and/or elect not to be supportive of their wife's career. Younger couples seek compatibility in a relationship. They do not wish to remain in a marriage where there is not respect, trust, love, and understanding just to meet society's expectations and to avoid the stigma of divorce.

The Indian community must recognize that the lack of financial dependence of Indian women on men is creating less economic need for marriage and a shift in the balance of power in marriage. Parents of teenagers and young adults must ask themselves whether the assumptions previous generations made still hold true, such as:

- Parents know best who would make an appropriate match for their child;

- Marrying someone from the same region and community in India is critical to a successful future; or

- Dating is bad because it calls into question one's character.

Parents must reflect on whether the manner in which they relate with their spouse and raise their children is having an adverse effect on the younger generations' views of marriage. Young adults must also reflect on whether Western culture is having an undue influence on how they perceive and value marriage.

The future success of the Indian family will not be because of destiny, duty, or following traditional Hindu customs. Instead, it will be the result of couples loving each other and having shared values, a commitment to each other, good communication, strong compatibility, and a willingness to collaborate through conflict. The book will explore these issues in an effort to help the older generations of Indians understand the younger generation's growing refusal to honor traditional marriage customs, and to empower younger generations of Indians to find a balance between the traditional customs and expectations of marriage and more contemporary needs and interests.

The Breakdown of the Hindu Marriage

Anjali and her husband Jay have been separated for three years after being married for seven. They have a handsome son, Arjun, who was conceived after years of trying. Jay now lives with his girl-friend, a divorcee with four children. She is the primary reason for his separation from Anjali. Arjun splits his time between his mother and father during the week and spends alternating weekends with each parent. Jay and Anjali no longer speak to each other directly, only through their respective attorneys.

Jay continues to have a key to their home, but when he visits, Anjali feels as though a stranger has entered. Standing in the presence of Jay causes Anjali fear and anxiety, in contrast to the happiness she once felt years ago. The police have been called to their home on more than one occasion, adding more fuel to the fire that is burning inside. Jay used to purchase beautiful jewelry for his wife, which she kept in a safe deposit box. After their separation, Jay lied to the bank, stating that he lost the safe deposit keys. He had a hole drilled in the safe deposit box, removed all its contents, and closed the account without informing Anjali. Now Anjali must provide a description and picture of each piece of jewelry if she wishes to regain access to it. Anjali laments that reliving her past by looking through old photo albums for pictures of happier times when she wore this jewelry is just not worth the pain. So Anjali sacrifices her jewelry, as she has so many other aspects of her once stable life.

Money was no object to Jay in making his wife and son happy. Now, Jay and Anjali fight over the allocation of even $100. Jay pays the expenses of his girlfriend, who travels to Australia to visit her children. He resents having to pay child support for his son Arjun and spousal support for Anjali, who is unemployed but who helped him throughout the early years of their marriage in building his lucrative businesses. Jay cannot understand why Anjali continues to demand more money through her lawyer, as well as equal access to his hard-earned property. Jay seeks to hurt Anjali by gaining brownie points with his son and tries to identify fault in Anjali's parenting, even at the expense of his son. For example, once when Anjali had gone to take an ill neighbor to the emergency room, Jay dropped in to visit his son. Not finding Anjali at home, he ranted and raved about her irresponsibility in leaving Arjun home alone and declared that he would notify his attorney of her negligence. He did not allow his son to explain where his mother went, and he bore the burden of his father's wrath, fearing the repercussions for his mother. The only winners in this situation are Jay and Angali's attorneys, who will profit from the couple's continuing inability to communicate or reach consensus on important financial matters and parenting responsibilities. The biggest loser in this fight is Arjun, who is being torn apart emotionally in this battle between his parents.

THE STORY OF JAY AND ANJALI IS NOT AN ABERRATION. Increasingly, Indian marriages are struggling, both in India and abroad. What has happened to the sacred Indian marriage? Where have the ideals of love, trust, and commitment gone? Did they ever exist, or were obedience, submissiveness, and fear on the part of the wife disguised as these more lofty principles? There is no doubt that when Jay and Anjali were married, their families had high hopes of a joyous and prosperous future for the couple.

I believe the decline of their marriage, as in many other Indian marriages, is due in part to:

1. Largely impractical premises of the arranged marriage system;

2. Traditionally inequitable gender roles;

3. Ineffective communication; and

4. Lack of collaborative problem-solving skills.

An exploration of each of these areas may help those considering an arranged marriage for their children or themselves assess whether this model is the most appropriate today. In addition, if a couple is in a marriage that is not working, whether it was an arranged marriage or love marriage, this discussion may provide some guidance on how to redirect the marital relationship in a more positive way.

The Significance of the Vedic Marriage

To understand how the Indian marriage has evolved, it is important to review its origins and basic premises. In Hinduism, there are sixteen important rights of passage (*samskaras*) in life. The word samskara is derived from the word *samskri*, which means to purify or form perfectly. The words *samskriti* (civilization) and *samskrit* (the perfect language) are also derived from the same root. The samskaras evolved over thousands of years as the disciplined stepping-stones to refinement or a perfect way to progress from stage to stage in this life and to help with a good future birth. The samskaras are fire rituals prescribed in the Vedas that mark various milestones in a human being's life. *Vivaha*, or marriage, is one of the sixteen samskaras that are to be observed by Hindus.

Vivaha is a sacrament that must be solemnized in accordance with Vedic rituals. The eighty-fifth *Sukta* of the tenth *Mandala* of the *Rig Veda* is known as the Marriage-Sukta, and the first Sukta of the fourteenth *Kanda* of *Artharva Veda* describes marriage. It is through the combination of these Vedic hymns that sages formulated the rituals of marriage in the *Grihya Sutras*. The marriage ceremony qualifies the husband to perform Vedic rituals and entitles the wife to participate in and benefit from her husband's rituals. Together, the husband and wife enter the grahastha (householder's) stage of life and pursue artha (material goods) and kama (pleasure and desires) while maintaining and upholding dharma (good conduct). The marriage ceremony is elaborate and consists of many stages, including a *homa* (fire). After the homa, the couple will take seven steps around the fire. Each step represents a prayer for harmony, love, good health, cooperation, wealth, children, and joy (Pandya 31):

1. Together, we promise to share the duties and responsibilities of our married life. We will take care of each other's well being, both material and spiritual.

2. Together, we will fill our hearts with strength and courage to share each other's joys and sorrows. Together we will protect and provide for our family.

3. Together, we have taken an oath of trust and loyalty to each other. We believe this will ensure prosperity, joy of life, and longevity. Our great standards of morality will allow us to raise children with noble character.

4. Together, we will develop a love for beauty, art, literature and will fill each other's life with the pursuit of human values including: love, compassion, understanding, sacrifice, and service.

5. Together, let us reconfirm our vows of purity, love, family duties, harmony, and spiritual values.

6. Together, we will conduct our lives according to the principles of dharma. We will ensure the continuation of our great Hindu heritage for the benefit of all humanity.

7. Together, with these seven steps, we will remain lifelong partners in matrimony and our bond is eternal. Let our love and friendship become eternal.

The Hindu marriage is considered an unbreakable bond between two souls. Some Hindus believe that the relationship extends up to seven lives. In Hinduism, the institution of marriage is not limited to humans. The gods are also ritually re-married to their divine consorts on a periodic basis in temples around the world, exemplifying the ideals of marriage. In the Hindu faith, one purpose of marriage is to produce good progeny and continue life on earth. Another purpose is to uphold social order and Hindu dharma. The married couple must work together in their quest for spiritual enlightenment, which can be attained by performing their obligatory duties and acquiring good karma (actions).

Mr. Jayaram V., an author of several books on Hinduism and founder of the website Hinduwebsite.com, in his on-line article entitled "Hindu Marriages Purpose and Significance" states:

> *Marriage in Hinduism, therefore, is not just a mutual contract between two individuals or a relationship of convenience, but a social contract and moral expediency, in which the couple agree to live together and share their*

lives, doing their respective duties, to keep the divine order and the institution of marriage intact. As the torch bearers of Hindu dharma, in their capacity as individual souls, whose destinies are intertwined by their previous karmas, married couples have a responsibility towards their society, the gods, other living beings and their ancestors. In short, in Hinduism, marriage is a social and family obligation to perpetuate a divine centered life in which self-realization rather than sexual gratification is the reason for its continuation.

The marriage rituals have another unique dimension. Mr. Jayaram V. explains that marriage is not merely a human affair, but a sacred covenant between a man and a woman in which the gods participate as witnesses and facilitate the transfer of the bride to the groom. During the marriage ceremony, the priest first marries the bride to the gods and then presents her to the groom as a gift from the gods. The groom is then asked to take an oath, with the gods as witnesses, that he will protect his bride and stay by her side for the rest of her life. The implication is that the husband should respect his wife and treat her as a divine gift. A man cannot complete his duties as a householder without his wife.

Thus, the purpose of marriage in the Indian culture is to fulfill a key rite of passage, to maintain divine order, to support the family unit and community, and to seek spiritual salvation. These religious premises explain why Hindu marriage remains such an important institution in Indian society. It also clarifies why India continues to have the lowest divorce rate in the world. Devout Hindus to this day refuse to dishonor the sacred vows of marriage out of respect for the auspicious rituals performed during the wedding ceremony. The commitment the couple makes during the wedding ceremony is blessed not only by the community and family, but by God, and it must be revered. To end the marriage sacrament would be akin to blasphemy and is avoided at all cost.

The Arranged Marriage Process

The predominant method by which Hindus marry is through an arrangement planned by parents of the bride and groom. Arranged marriages have been part of the Indian culture since the fourth century. The system of arranged marriage involves parents being actively engaged in the exploration of potential partners for their children and in the final decision of whom they will marry.

For centuries Indians have been raised to make a lifelong commitment—mentally, emotionally, and spiritually—to the person their parents identify to be their spouse. Young adults did not dare fall in love and give their heart to someone before marriage because they knew that to do so would be fruitless, lead to a broken heart, and be considered sacrilegious. Their partner could only be the person they were destined to marry based on their horoscope and past karma. It would be the duty of their parents, as instruments of God, working with trusted family and key members of the community, to carefully identify the most appropriate partner for them according to traditional customs. The concept of dating or personal involvement in the selection of a spouse is inconsistent with this time-honored approach, as it would create the possibility of people falling in love and disobeying their parents' wishes, and it could endanger the virginity and chastity of young women, a virtue fiercely guarded by parents of daughters.

The arranged marriage model began when the ritual of child marriage prevailed in India. Child marriages were performed to restrict children from marrying outside their community and social status. The practice was essentially a way of uniting and maintaining the difference between the rich upper class and the poor lower class. The practice of arranged marriage continues to serve many purposes, including: 1) the assurance for parents that their children will be married; 2) the confidence for parents that as a result of prescreening, the match selected for their child is appropriate in terms of caste, education, character, and family status; 3) the preservation and continuation of the family lineage; 4) the possible extension of the family property by alliances with a wealthier family; and 5) the potential connection with a family of greater status, which lends prestige and could be beneficial when matters requiring influence arise (Rao, 15).

While the system of arranged marriages began as a way of uniting and maintaining upper-caste families, it eventually spread to the lower castes, where it is used for the same purpose. Though the specifics of how arranged marriages are coordinated may vary from region to region, marriage throughout India is considered an alliance between two families rather than just the union between two individuals. Notwithstanding the hundreds of Bollywood movies that portray love marriages as the norm, 90 percent of all Indian marriages are arranged.

As it is critically important to Indian families that their children marry, many parents begin marriage preparations when their children are young, with the assistance of friends, family, or marriage brokers who identify suitable matches in the community. The age, family, home, health, and nature of the prospective bride and groom are considered carefully. The characteristics that are evaluated include character and behavior, intellectual maturity, form and beauty, and qualities such as non-violence, honesty, gratitude, and kindness.

A trusted matchmaker is often used by families to gain information on an array of possible matches. The matchmaker reviews the family background, economic status, general character, family reputation, dowry value, the effect of the alliance on property, and other matters in determining who would be a suitable match. In North America, newspapers like *India Abroad*, websites such as shaadi.com or vivahabandhan.com, and national or regional social events such as the conference conducted by the Association of Kannada Kootas of America or the Telugu Association of Northern America serve as modern-day matchmakers. Indian families in metropolitan cities around the world use social networking and technology as a way of bridging distances and meeting potential partners.

In India, once a match is found, a meeting is arranged during which the two families convene and the boy and girl see each other. In the past, girls were asked to sing or play an instrument in an effort to demonstrate their unique talents. Additionally, girls were often examined for physical deformities and questioned on their ability to cook and do household chores. Today, the boy and girl are often given an opportunity to speak with each other. Once the young man, young woman, and their families agree on the union, representatives of the two families meet with a priest to discuss the compatibility of the birth stars of the boy and girl, as well as the date, time, and location of the wedding. If the priest notes that their horoscopes are incompatible, the union is generally cancelled.

Indians have used the system of arranged marriage for centuries because it has several advantages, including the assurance for parents that their daughter will have a mate who offers her financial security and stability. The couple will have a common language, customs, foods, and traditions, which they will ideally preserve for future generations. The couple will also enjoy the support and guidance of both families as they endeavor to begin a life together. All Indian parents pray for their children to enjoy a wonderful married life with a partner who will make them happy. Parents have historically used a variety of factors to assist them in making that critical determination of who would be the most suitable match for their child.

The Criteria Used for Partner Selection in Arranged Marriages

The traditional criteria upon which parental selection of a suitable partner for their child was based included such factors as caste, horoscope, dowry, language (region), and family status. While the system of arranged marriage has survived over the centuries, in recent decades the inequities of this system are more evident. A brief overview of these criteria is helpful to understand their relevance today.

Caste

A caste system is a division of society based on labor and family lineage. In India there are four castes arranged in a hierarchy. The word for caste is *Varna*. Each Varna has certain duties and rights. Each Varna's members have to work in a certain occupation that only those Varna members are allowed to perform. Each Varna also has a certain diet. The highest Varna is the *Brahmin*. Members of this class are priests and the educated people of the society. The next Varna in the hierarchy is *Kshatriya*. The members of this class are the rulers, warriors, and aristocrats of the society. Next are the *Vaishya*, who serve as the landlords and businessmen of the society. Then there are the *Sudras*, who are the farmers and working class of the society. Below these castes are the *Dhalits*, untouchables, who work in the most undesirable jobs such as cleaning and sewage.

Each Varna—and also the untouchables—is divided into many communities. These communities are called *Jaatis*. Each Jaati is limited to professions worthy of its Varna. Each Jaati is limited to the Varna diet, and historically Jaati members are allowed to marry only their Jaati members. People are born into their Jaati, and it cannot be changed. Indians have always respected this rule regarding marriage, and those who dared to break the rule were deemed outcastes.

In essence, the arranged marriage system in India is a way of maintaining the caste system. It has been a tool for the upper-caste people to protect their community and to preserve their social status. As such, wealthy families married their children to a person of the same caste or same social background. This practice eventually passed on to the lower castes as well, where it has been used for the same purpose. Many Indian families continue striving to ensure that their children marry within the same caste and Jaati; they do this by restricting the choice of potential partners to those from the same caste and Jaati.

Many Indians, including Mahatma Gandhi, have rebuked the caste system. It is inconsistent with the Hindu concepts of universal respect, brotherhood, and peace, as well as the belief that God resides in the soul of every human being. Today, many Indians reject the caste system and believe there is no reason to perpetuate caste distinctions through the institution of marriage. Indians in India and around the world, of all castes and Jaatis, have achieved high levels of education and excellent jobs. Indians no longer restrict their education, work, or ambitions to fields related to their caste. Similarly, many Indians today do not wish to limit their search for a potential life partner to someone from the same caste or Jaati.

 In lieu of considering caste or Jaati as an important selection criteria for a life partner, an Indian parent or a young adult instead may consider traits that are more relevant today than what caste historically represented. For example, if caste guaranteed a particular diet, such as vegetarianism, then that can be noted as an important consideration by a young adult when meeting others. If caste represents the level of education one seeks in a life partner, then education goals can be discussed. If caste represents adherence to particular customs that are deemed key criteria for compatibility, such as regular visits to the temple or observation of special fasts, then they should be considered. Caste in and of itself is likely to be a low, or non-existent, priority for this and future generations of Indians. Younger generations, particularly those who have moved abroad, often do not even know what their caste is. However, the values or customs that caste represented in India for decades could continue to be considered carefully for their relevance in the pursuit of a suitable spouse today.

Horoscope

Indian astrology is the study of planetary movements and their influence on human beings. As marriage is the most sacred event for Hindus, great care is taken before entering into marriage. Indians share a unanimous desire to have a happy and prosperous married life. It is believed that horoscope matchmaking is required before marriage to ensure selection of a perfect life partner and to guarantee a successful married life. The use of Indian astrology in horoscope matching is considered an art and is believed to predict difficult situations or emotions that couples may face in the future. The matchmaking of horoscopes informs families about whether the married couple will lead a life filled with hardships and predicts the amount of love between the couple, the mutual understanding between the partners, and their sexual compatibility. If horoscopes are not matched properly, it is believed that the couple will lead an unhappy life, will experience many problems, and may eventually die or divorce.

Many Indian families do not start any important activity, business, or relationship without consulting an astrologer. While many Indians are still convinced of the value in the information gleaned from horoscopes, the use of astrologers and their credibility has declined. For example, when I agreed to marry my husband, a renowned astrologer reviewed our horoscopes. He stated that we would not be compatible and I should not marry him. While I did not yet know my husband, I was disappointed to hear this news and dreaded having to renew my search for a suitable groom. The next evening, my father met with yet another astrologer, who said that our horoscopes were fine and there was no reason that we should not marry. My parents obviously followed the advice of the second astrologer. Given this experience, I am dubious about the use of astrologers. Most of the couples I know who have divorced or are in the process of getting divorced had their horoscopes approved as a good match by some astrologer before they got married. I do not believe an astrologer's approval is a guarantee or even an essential ingredient for success in marriage.

 The purpose of matching horoscopes is to ensure compatibility. Today, it is far more effective for a young couple to meet directly; spend quality time together; learn about each others' personalities, character, values, likes, dislikes, and goals. Why depend on paying a complete stranger to interpret handwritten notes scribbled on paper decades earlier by another priest? The couple themselves are in a position in the present to far more ably determine their compatibility. The interest in consulting an astrologer, the likelihood of finding a trusted astrologer, and the perceived need among younger generations to compare horoscopes prior to marrying is diminishing. Many Indian children born abroad never even have a horoscope prepared when they are born. Parents who believe strongly in the power of the planets may have to learn to instead trust the impressions, feelings, and instincts of their children in assessing the compatibility of potential partners. As will be discussed later, in Chapter III, compatibility can be explored and assessed quite effectively through candid discussions, precluding the reliance on horoscopes.

The Breakdown of the Hindu Marriage

Dowry

Dowry is the payment in cash and/or kind by the bride's family to the bridegroom's family, along with the giving away of the bride (*Kanyadaan*) in the Indian marriage. Dowry originated in upper-caste families as a wedding gift to the bride from her family. Dowry was also given to provide for the bride should something unfortunate happen to her husband, such as death. The dowry system became a tool for "enhancing family social status and economic worth" (Rao 61). Author Prakasa Rao notes five purposes of the dowry: it (1) provides an occasion for people to boost their self-esteem through feasts and displays of material objects; (2) makes alliances with the families of similar status; (3) helps prevent the breakup of family property; (4) gets a better match for daughters; (5) furnishes daughters with some kind of social and economic security (Rao 61-62). The expensive nature of dowries has served to raise the marriage age in the middle and lower caste because families have not been able to meet dowry demands, and it has also forced some families "to transcend their caste groups and find bridegrooms from other sub caste and different caste" (Rao 62).

There are several disadvantages to dowries. Families may suffer financial hardships due to the exorbitant nature of dowries. They may not be able to afford dowries, therefore preventing their children from marriage, causing "girls to occasionally commit suicide in order to rid their fathers of financial burdens" (Rao 62). Because of instances like these, many consider "the dowry system as a social evil and an intolerable burden to many brides' families" (Rao 62).

As a result, the Dowry Prohibition Act of 1961 was passed. It decrees, "to give, take, or demand a dowry is an offense punishable by imprisonment and fines" (Diwan 77). A dowry is also defined as "any property or valuable security given or agreed to be given either directly or indirectly by one party to a marriage to the other party to the marriage, or by the parents of either party to a marriage or by any other person, to either party to the marriage or to any other person at or before or after the marriage as consideration for the marriage of the said parties" (Diwan 77). The law does make the following exclusion: "any presents made at the time of marriage to either party to the marriage in the form of cash, ornament, clothes or other articles, do not count as a dowry" (Diwan 77). These items are considered wedding gifts. The law does create the following loophole: "the giving or taking of dowry does not affect the validity of the marriage.... [I]f the dowry is given, the bride is entitled to it, but the person giving it is punished by law if discovered" (Diwan 77). Although the dowry was legally prohibited in 1961, it continues to be highly used. The groom often demands a dowry consisting of money, cars, jewelry, furniture, or electronics. If a family does not offer a significant dowry, the girl is unlikely to have a "good" match. A good match for a very poor family might be marriage of their daughter into a slightly better situated family, and a good match for a middle-income family might be finding a husband who is a doctor or engineer. When the dowry is not considered sufficient or is not forthcoming, the bride is often harassed and made miserable.

Smitha is a young, well-educated, and beautiful young woman in Bangalore. Smitha's parents were delighted when Vijay and his family approached them for her hand in marriage. Vijay is a well-established software engineer in Washington, DC, and Smitha's parents believed she would have a wonderful life with Vijay. Vijay's parents placed incredible demands on Smitha's parents for a large dowry. They insisted on receiving a great deal of cash, a new home for their son in Bangalore, and a certain quantity of jewelry for Smitha. Smitha's middle-class parents took out loans and stretched to their maximum potential to meet the requests. They did not want to jeopardize their daughter's future because of financial challenges. Vijay began physically and verbally abusing Smita in India soon after they were married. Smitha did not tell her parents anything, as she knew how hard they had worked to get her married and how hopeful they were for her happiness. Smitha prayed that things would improve when she and Vijay came to the United States. Unfortunately, they only got worse. Vijay continued to abuse Smitha and made demands for more money from her parents. He did not let Smitha leave their apartment and monitored her conversations with her family. Smitha managed to escape to a neighbor's apartment when Vijay was at work, and she is planning to return to India as soon as possible. She has been married less than three months, and her parents have spent their life savings on her wedding and dowry.

Dowry-related abuse can escalate to the point where the husband or his family burns the bride. The official count of these incidents is low because the family often reports them as accidents or suicides. Statistics found in several Internet articles are disturbing. In Delhi, a woman is burned to death almost every twelve hours. In 1988, 2,209 women were killed in dowry-related incidents, and in 1990, 4,835 were killed. The lack of official reporting of this crime is apparent in Delhi, where 90 percent of cases of burnt women were recorded as accidents, 5 percent as suicide, and only the remaining 5 percent were listed as murder. According to Indian government figures, there were a total of 5,377 dowry deaths in 1993, an increase of

12 percent from 1992. Despite a rigorous 1986 amendment to the Indian Penal Code (IPC) to prevent dowry deaths, convictions are rare, and judges are often uninterested and susceptible to bribery.

 Like many customs, time has altered the need for the dowry. The young couple, if well educated and employed, will not need to rely on a dowry for security. If a dowry is given, more often than not, it gets absorbed into the groom's household for the good of the entire family. A dowry should not be a prerequisite for a couple to marry. Parents who demand a dowry to give their son's hand in marriage do a disservice to their child, as they may be limiting or excluding women from consideration who have a great deal to offer their son in terms of compatibility and companionship. The use of dowries today makes women feel like property to be sold for a price. Gifts to children to support them when they are beginning their life together are one thing, but it is degrading in the eyes of a young woman for her parents to have to pay for the groom and his family to accept her hand in marriage. Money cannot buy a couple's happiness. Where dowries are given or accepted, they have often proven to be a future source of contention either because the wife resents that her parents had to spend such a hefty sum on her marriage or because the husband feels that the wife's family did not give him enough money. Parents today should recognize the inappropriateness of a requesting or paying a dowry and completely eliminate it as a factor in identifying a suitable match for their child.

Language

The Indian constitution recognizes eighteen official languages of the country. There are also 1,600 regional dialects. Historically, families selected partners for their child from the same region. This ensured a common language, food, and customs. For Indians who have left India, maintaining fluency in their mother tongue is challenging. Parents often speak their native language at home, yet the strong influence of TV and school overwhelmingly shift a child's focus to proficiency in English. For years I tried to learn how to read and write in Kannada, my native language, during summer holidays. I practiced the alphabet with great discipline and effort, but as soon as school resumed, my new language skills disappeared because they were not used. To this day I cannot read or write in Kannada, yet this has in no in way limited my ability to enjoy the company of other Indians, to practice the Hindu faith, or to communicate effectively with my husband, who, unlike me, speaks Kannada fluently and was raised in India.

 Hindi and English are the primary languages of India. For Indians who live outside of India, and even for many who live in India, English is the primary language. Each time I visit Bangalore and speak in Kannada, people respond in English. The need for fluency in an Indian language is less necessary for effective communication between a couple, particularly a couple living abroad, because of the universality of English. This does not mean that preserving native languages is not important. In fact, many Indians are bilingual or trilingual. However, limiting the search for a future partner to individuals who share the same native language is not practical or necessary to ensure good communication. A couple can always agree to continue to speak their respective native language with their family, strive to learn each other's native language, and pass both native languages on to their children.

Family Status and Background

An important consideration for Indian parents is the type of family the bride and groom come from. The thinking is that people from families with wealth, strong values, and a good reputation, are more likely to be decent people. Parents believe that their child will be well taken care of if they marry into a good family. Historically, brides in India would move in with their husband and his family after marriage, so it was even more crucial that the parents felt comfortable with the family their daughter would be joining and that the parents of the groom believed that their new daughter-in-law would be a good fit in the family. When I went to India to meet young men who had been prescreened by my father, most of them were from wealthy families. My relatives always emphasized the value of marrying *up*. If I were to marry someone from a more recognized family it would bring my whole family honor and prestige. We would gain access to special connections in local government. We would have business advantages and opportunities. I personally did not care about the family status of the young men I met. I noticed that those from more privileged backgrounds tended to be arrogant, snobbish, and self absorbed. I felt as though my only purpose was to provide them with a one-way ticket to the United States.

As an up-and-coming lawyer who would continue to live in the United States, not in India, I knew that connections with a wealthy family in India would not give me any real advantage. What was more important to me was the kind of person my future husband was. It is often the case that children are nothing like their parents. Just because a family or parents are well-known and possess positive qualities, these traits may not necessarily be passed down to their children. Similarly, parents or families that are less than perfect can raise children who are kind, intelligent, and talented. I married a man from a middle-class family that had a reputation for honesty and hard work. My in-laws' willingness to allow their eldest son to marry me, leave India, and pursue his career goals, as well as their affection and open-mindedness toward me, are all that I have ever needed.

The Breakdown of the Hindu Marriage

> Focusing solely on family status can lead to disastrous results. Take the case of Arun and Priya. Arun was a lower-middle-class groom who married a woman because of her family's wealth and upper-class status. While Arun had no wealth to speak of, he did have a good education and he lived in the United States, which is why Priya's parents agreed to let her marry him. Arun worked hard, got a good job, and tried his best to give his wife all the comforts in the world. He paid for and supported her higher education as well. Unfortunately, Priya was never satisfied and often complained that they did not live in a big house or enjoy a wealthier lifestyle. She loved to buy expensive clothes, shoes, and jewelry. Arun complained constantly about her reckless spending and privately resented that her parents did not aid him in supporting her extravagant lifestyle. Priya ridiculed Arun for his poor, unsophisticated background and often said disrespectful things about his family. Arun's decision to marry based primarily on family status contributed to his leading a very difficult life.

 Parents today must consider the purpose of evaluating a family's status and background in selecting a suitable match for their child. Ideally, marriage is a union of two families, not just two individuals. A wealthy or high-status family is not necessarily a better family than a happy, caring, and supportive middle-class family. As a parent, it is more important that a family treats your child well and loves him or her— not how big or fancy the family's home is.

To many young Indians, particularly those from educated families and families that have moved abroad, the premises of the arranged marriage system are generally no longer relevant considerations. Those premises are to preserve the caste system;

37

to ensure that the match is appropriate in terms of caste, horoscope, family background, dowry, language, and customs; and the possible opportunity to connect with a family of greater status. These factors were important in the past largely because women were not educated and thus depended upon their husband for lifelong support. Marrying into a family that was wealthy and finding a groom that was well educated was important for parents to ensure their daughter's future security. Parents saved for years to provide their daughter with a large dowry in the hopes of attracting the most sought-after groom, and they prayed that the horoscopes supported the liaison. Cultural norms dictated that families married within their caste. Due to limited mobility, families restricted their search for a potential groom to young people within their community.

Today, of course, many women are independent, well educated, and financially secure. They do not need to rely on a well-established husband for their well-being. People are far more mobile, routinely travelling throughout India as well as around the world. Young Indians do not identify with a particular language or region of India in the same way that previous generations did. The expectation of similar caste, customs, or food is less important to young adults because marriage serves a completely different purpose today—that of providing companionship and love. Given the shift in the purpose of marriage, the factors that should be considered in selecting an appropriate partner have far less to do with caste, horoscope, or family status and much more to do with character, personality, values, and goals.

Consequences of Forcing an Arranged Marriage

Indian parents often preclude their child from interacting with people of the opposite gender in an effort to keep them free of attachments and pure in their heart in anticipation of a future arranged marriage. Limiting or denying interaction with the opposite sex often engenders curiosity and resentment. Many Indian parents fear that if their child becomes too friendly with a person of the opposite gender, the child will get inappropriate ideas and take the relationship beyond a platonic friendship. This demonstrates a lack of trust between the parent and child. Parents should emphasize and discuss the values of personal integrity, self-respect, and good character with their children. These values can be maintained while simultaneously having healthy relationships with members of the opposite sex. When children are prohibited from interacting with the opposite gender, it creates desire and interest in the unknown and forbidden.

On my visits to India as a teenager I noticed a very odd behavior among young men. When walking along crowded sidewalks, in busy shopping areas, in parks, or even in movie theaters, young men often bumped and rubbed up against me and other young women. It was as though they were desperate to achieve some connection with a member of the opposite sex. Catcalling and teasing of young women by men in India is commonplace. I very rarely observed young men and women having a respectful conversation in India, unless they were related. I know that this dynamic has changed in recent years, particularly in more urban parts of India and among educated young adults. It is only through respectful and collegial conversations that young men and women can develop their social skills and a sense of confidence with the opposite sex. The characteristics they find attractive and desirable in a future life partner can be gleaned through these interactions, and, ideally, one day they will meet a person who embodies their perfect match.

When I was in law school, I had an Indian friend who grew up in a very strict home environment. As a result, when she was in college, she greatly enjoyed her freedom from parental oversight. She wore tight clothes and far too much makeup, drank heavily, and stayed out until the early hours of the morning. She had several boyfriends and was taking full advantage of her newfound freedom. I believe that if she had been given the opportunity while growing up to have boys as friends and a social life with limits, she may not have rebelled so strongly when she left home for the first time.

Giving up the historically sound criteria used in selecting a suitable match—such as caste, family status, and language—and the tried and true traditions associated with arranged marriages—such as the use of horoscopes and dowry—is very difficult for older generations of Indians. When young adults refuse to honor these criteria in their selection of a partner, it is perceived as very disrespectful and often becomes the source of great conflict between parents and children. When parents force their children to adopt the traditional arranged marriage model, it can often lead to disastrous results for the couple.

Marriage for young Indian adults is an important life decision, not just a duty or a rite of passage. When Indian parents force their children to marry someone they do not wish to marry it can often lead to terrible results.

Puja is the oldest of five children, born and raised in India. A respected member of the community, impressed by her character, was interested in having her marry his son. Puja's parents, out of respect for this gentleman, his family, and his standing in the community, agreed to the marriage proposal.

Vikram, born and raised in India, had moved to the United States for higher studies. He had a great job in the IT industry and had also fallen in love with a woman in the United States. He did not know how to break the news of his relationship to his parents, so he didn't. He put off his parents' requests that he marry as long as he could, until finally during a visit to India he conceded and married Puja. He and Puja had a grand wedding, but within months of Puja joining Vikram in the United States, things changed. Vikram did not speak or interact with his wife. He ignored her to such an extent that Puja finally left Vikram. After years of heartache, stress, anger, frustration, and desperate attempts at trying to understand what happened to their marriage, Puja ultimately agreed to divorce Vikram. Vikram and Puja are now happily remarried to new partners. If Vikram had just had the courage to explain to his parents that he loved another person and did not wish to marry Puja, he would have avoided years of pain and suffering for himself, Puja, and their families.

Another very common scenario is for parents to force their daughter to marry at a young age to avoid the risk that she may not marry, that she will fall in love, or that she will want to marry someone that does not meet the family's expectations.

Devi got married immediately after graduating from high school. Her parents were afraid that as a beautiful young woman she would be influenced by Western culture and begin dating boys or possibly even fall in love. To prevent such temptation, Devi's marriage to Raj was quickly arranged. Raj, who had grown up in India, joined Devi in the United States and did not approve of her clothes or her lifestyle. He expected her to prepare fresh Indian food for each meal, to dress in a sari, and to limit her time with friends outside the home. Devi resented her new responsibilities. She wanted to go to college, keep her social life, and enjoy her youth. She was frustrated by Raj's dependence on her and his unwillingness to adapt to the American way of life. She divorced Raj within a year of their marriage. Since then Devi has gone to college and medical school, become a doctor, remarried, and made a beautiful family. She is very happy today. If Devi's parents had just trusted her to make good decisions and to marry when she was ready, she might not have had to endure the traumatic experience of a failed marriage at the tender age of eighteen.

Arranged Marriages to NRIs

The scenario of Devi and Raj or even Puja and Vijay follows another recurring theme in arranged marriages: arranged marriages between Indian men or women and NRIs (non-resident Indians). In recent years, there has been a growing trend for parents in India to get their son or daughter married to NRIs, hoping the marriage will provide the opportunity to settle in a foreign country and guarantee a better life. Particularly in the 1980s and 1990s, Indian men and women living in the United States routinely returned to India to find a spouse either on their own accord or at the insistence of their parents. The parents of young men and women in India would be excited to give their child's hand in marriage to someone settled abroad. It was prestigious to have a son- or daughter-in-law from America. The desire to go abroad was so immense that parents would marry their children off to suitors from another country, regardless of how much dowry was expected, how large the age difference between the young man and woman might be, or how physically incompatible the couple seemed.

Compatibility can be an issue even between two people born and raised in the same country. If one of the partners in the marriage has lived a large part of his or her life in the United States, Europe or somewhere else outside India, it creates yet one more layer of differences that must be worked through when marrying someone born and raised in India. Statistics suggest that 225 women from metropolitan cities in India get married to NRIs every year, and of these, almost 25 are either deserted by their husbands or wish to end their marriage due to reasons of incompatibility or deception.

The deception could be that the NRI husband already has another wife, and in some cases children also, settled with him abroad. In many cases, the groom does not take the bride with him, leaving her behind with either his or her parents. Sometimes, the NRI spouse often exaggerates his possessions in the foreign country, such as the value of his home and car. He might represent that he has a high-paying job, but in actuality he might not be in a position to support a family after marriage. Often, the lifestyle of the NRI spouse is too Western for the Indian spouse to keep pace. The NRI spouse often feels that the new bride or groom is not a suitable partner and seeks a divorce on the grounds of incompatibility.

There is a saying in India that you must tell a thousand lies to make a marriage happen. This is actually not far from the truth. Often, parents, friends, family, and marriage brokers exaggerate the truth or misrepresent information in order to create a marital alliance. This may include what type of education or job the bridegroom has, the financial status of a family, or even whether the young man or young woman smokes or drinks. A more frequent misrepresentation concerns whether a young man or woman has had a previous relationship. Historically, an Indian woman's virginity is sacred. If a woman has had a relationship with a man, she is considered to be tainted and of bad character. As a result, if a young woman has had a past relationship with a man, this information is generally covered up and not discussed. Similarly, a young man's prior relationships with women are generally not shared with the bride before marriage. When a young man or young woman has not terminated a previous relationship and feels forced into a new alliance, that new alliance is likely to fail. The arranged marriage system forces young people to pretend that prior relationships are unimportant and pressures them into entering a new relationship with the hope that the new partner will help past loves be forgotten. These past relationships often come up again during a marriage and can be the source of tremendous friction, heartache, and, finally, divorce.

 Choosing a husband or wife solely based on caste, language, wealth, region, horoscope, or dowry, as Indian parents have for decades, is illogical today. While historically it has been important for Indian parents that their children, particularly daughters, remain chaste, avoid a bad reputation by remaining unmarried beyond the age of twenty-six, and marry *up*, parents should recognize that their interest in what society thinks or preserving the family lineage should not outweigh their child's happiness. If a person is not ready mentally or emotionally to commit to marriage, parents should not force it. If they do, they risk ruining the lives of not only one but two young people. Marriages of convenience; marriages to increase wealth or status; marriages to enable migration abroad; marriages to keep wealth within the family; marriages to ensure that a girl is married young, before she is tempted to fall in love or lose her virginity; marriages to ensure that the family name is carried on; marriages to meet society's expectations; or marriages because of promises made to friends or family—do not produce healthy, happy, and long-lasting marriages today.

II

Imbalanced Gender Roles

A S YOUNG INDIAN ADULTS CONTEMPLATE MARRIAGE, ONE
consideration they weigh heavily is expectations in
marriage. Young Indians observe the marital relationship
of their parents and those around them in determining the nature
of and expectations in the traditional Indian marriage. In observing the conduct of their parents and other elders in the Indian
community, Indian youth often make the assumption that if
they marry an Indian, he or she will behave just as their parents
behave, and this could lead to a miserable life.

There are a number of negative stereotypes of Indian men, as
India is traditionally a patriarchal society. Some examples of
the behavioral characteristics of Indian men that young Indian
women fear include:

1. **The Belittler** – This is the husband who always talks down
to his wife and tells her either directly or indirectly that she is
stupid or incompetent. This husband assumes that his wife does
not have the intelligence to engage in conversation about important family decisions, such as the purchase of a car, moving to a
new city, or buying a home. Any time the wife tries to provide
input or feedback, the husband shuts her down immediately. The
husband tramps down her feelings regularly, without regard. He
makes her feel inadequate and unworthy. The low self-esteem
this behavior creates has a tremendously negative impact on the

health and happiness of the wife. Daughters in such a household will hate Indian men, and if they marry, they want nothing more than to marry a man from any other race. Some sons from such a household will grow up feeling very sorry for their mother. Other sons, however, grow up to be just as arrogant as their father and believe that this is how a man should treat his wife.

2. **The Criticizer** – This husband is a close cousin of the belittler. The criticizer complains about everything his wife does. She cannot prepare a single meal without some type of negative comment: there is not enough salt, this is too spicy, you didn't add enough sugar, this doesn't taste like my mother's cooking. The criticizer does not lend a hand to support his wife. He merely sits back and watches her work, then enjoys making remarks on her work once she is done. The clothes the wife wears are never appropriate for the occasion, the wife's makeup or hair is never nice enough, or the house is not kept sufficiently clean. This husband never apologizes when he makes a mistake. The word *sorry* is not in his vocabulary. He thinks that to admit fault would be denigrating and inappropriate given his status as the family's patriarch. In this situation, the wife ignores her husband's words and develops a tolerance for such criticism. She does not take his comments to heart, although she resents his constant nagging. She secretly curses her husband, hoping that in his next life he will be born a woman so she can have the opportunity to criticize him. Positive feedback or a kind word from the husband is a very rare occurrence. Girls born of this household feel denigrated by Indian men. Men growing up in this environment may think it is natural to make negative comments about their wife and never treat them as equals.

3. **The Controller** – This is the husband who makes all the decisions in the household and believes he is the king. The wife is not given financial independence. She must request money from her husband, often even for groceries. She is not permitted to

purchase anything for herself such as jewelry, shoes, or clothes, as the husband sees them as unnecessary extravagances and does not trust her to make good choices. The wife in this situation is limited in her authority to make spending decisions. She does not have the freedom to go out to lunch with friends or even buy gifts for her children. She cannot entertain guests without her husband's permission. She is not allowed to talk with men, even the husbands of her friends. Her husband watches her actions like a hawk. The wife generally is responsible for all cooking, cleaning, laundry, and household responsibilities. A girl growing up in this environment often does not want to get married—to any man. A boy growing up in this environment may have an exaggerated sense of self-confidence and ego.

Some aspects of these personality traits are seen in men in all races and cultures, but they are prevalent in Indian men. The stereotype that many Indian women carry with them by observing their father, grandfathers, or uncles is that Indian men are demanding, patronizing, self-centered, and difficult to live with or satisfy. As a result, many Indian women choose not to marry—or if they marry, they marry into a different race. To overcome these stereotypes, the younger generations of Indian men need to recognize the importance of equality among genders, respect, and sharing responsibilities in a marriage.

When I married my husband, several of my girlfriends were surprised, felt sorry for me, thought I was crazy, and were scared for my future. They all believed it was the wrong decision to marry an Indian man, especially one recently arrived from India, a FOB (fresh off the boat). An Indian man who had lived in America for a short time might have been slightly influenced by Western culture and have a bit of an open mind, but a man from India would clearly mean trouble. Amazingly, my husband is more open-minded and liberal than many men born and raised in the United States. I have always enjoyed the freedom to do and say as

I like and be the person I want to be. From my own experience, I believe that making broad generalizations about Indian men is unfair, even if it is based on years of experience or observation. As well, I know many Indian men I would have divorced within a week of marriage. Each person is unique, however, and possesses qualities that are both positive and negative. One must get to know a person before judging him or her. If being treated with respect, having equal voice and balance in a relationship, and financial independence are important to a woman, she should explore these issues with the men she meets and not assume all Indian men are the same.

Stereotypes of Indian women are equally commonplace and also contribute to a young Indian woman's trepidations regarding marriage. Many of these stereotypes come from ancient Hindu mythology. With all due respect to the ancient Hindu scriptures and the Hindu epics the *Mahabharatha* and *Ramayana*, the stories therein often portray an image of the Indian wife that exacerbates the stereotypical image. In the Hindu epic *Ramayana*, Princess Sita follows Lord Rama to live in the forest for fourteen years. She is kidnapped by the demon Ravana and lives in captivity with demons. Although she made great sacrifices for her husband, members of the community spread rumors about her chastity. When she and Lord Rama return home. Lord Rama, in order to quash these rumors, asks his brother Laxmana to abandon her in the forest. Lord Rama is considered the ideal husband, son, brother, and father in Hinduism. Yet, he listens to the ignorant discussions of the community laundry man who suggests that his wife was unfaithful while she lived under the care of Ravana. He continues to be suspicious and unforgiving even after Agni, the god of fire, proclaims to everyone that Sita is completely pure when she tries to burn herself and survives unscathed. The divine scriptures are intended to instruct mankind on appropriate behavior and values. If this instance had been used by Lord Rama to explain to the community the importance of trust in a relationship and to reinforce his love for and faith in his wife, the standing of women in India might have been enhanced. In the *Ramayana*, after being abandoned by her husband, Sita is taken in by a Sage and gives birth to two sons, Lava and Kusha. She never returns to Lord Rama, and in that act of defiance, I believe she maintains her self-respect and dignity. The stereotype of Indian women the *Ramayana* seeks to create is that they are obedient, but not to be trusted.

In the epic *Mahabharatha*, Draupadi allows herself to be shared as a wife by the five Pandava brothers because her mother-in-law, not knowing what prize her son Arjuna had won in a competition, told her son to "share whatever it was that he had won with his brothers." If Draupadi's dignity were to be respected, Arjuna would have explained to his mother that he would not share his new wife with his brothers. Later in the *Mahabharatha*, Draupadi is wagered like property by one of her husbands, Yudishtera, in a game of dice, and is lost. She is then forcibly disrobed by the evil Kauravas while her five husbands watch dejectedly. Fortunately, Draupadi's faith in Lord Krishna saves her from this cruelty.

In *Daksha Yagna*, Sati, wife of Lord Shiva, burns herself alive because of the manner in which her father disgraced her husband. It is from this story that we have named the modern practice of *sati*, in which widows burn themselves alive along with their deceased husband on the funeral pyre as the ultimate example of wifely devotion. Although the British banned sati, there have been several examples of sati in India in recent years. Sati highlights the chastity of women and their commitment to their husband, even after death. The alternative to sati has historically been forced widowhood. The life of a widow in India has been generally miserable, as she has had to take a position of degradation in the household and society. In India there was also an institution known as *Devdasi*, in which temples kept unmarried women as dancers or prostitutes. These women were "married" to god. This system enabled temples to earn income by engaging these women in immoral activities. Laws have been passed outlawing this practice as well. In the story of *Satya Harishchandra*, in an effort to preserve his reputation for truth, Harishchandra allows his wife to be sold in order to repay a debt. In the story of *Savitri*, Savitri follows Yama, the god of death, on a long journey and cleverly tricks him into bringing her husband back to life. In short, Indian mythology describes the primary purpose of the wife as completely focused on the service of her husband. To ensure his long life and success, she is always willing to sacrifice her health and happiness.

As in the case of Mother Sita, Indian women of my mother's generation and those in all previous generations were raised to defer to their husband. Women were generally not educated, except those in wealthier families. Indian women have long suffered a great deal of physical and emotional abuse at hands of their husbands and in-laws. They have lived lives of tremendous personal sacrifice and tolerated poor treatment on a daily basis. Regardless of their maltreatment, Indian women did not return to their parents' home or leave their husband, because to do so would bring shame upon their family. Many Indian men, even those living in North America, still believe that Indian women should be submissive and obey the commands of their husband, who is to be considered their god. In addition, women's primary responsibilities include caring for several children and maintaining a spic-and-span household. Indian men also expect Indian women to be excellent cooks and to prepare lavish meals for large groups of people in the blink of an eye. These expectations of Indian women, however, are no longer accurate, necessary, or acceptable.

Indian women today do not believe they are property, and the vast majority will no longer allow themselves to be treated as such. Indian women are as educated as—and in many instances more educated than—Indian men. The institution of marriage is no longer necessary for women to have economic security. Most young Indian women today will not bow down in deference to their husband and do whatever he asks. Many women want to pursue careers, and some do not want children. Some do not know how to cook and refuse to clean because they were raised in homes with servants, are not accustomed to cleaning, or have careers that preclude the time for domestic chores.

 The generalizations that Indian men are arrogant and controlling and Indian women are meek and submissive are not always true. In addition, the assumptions that men will work outside the home and women will cook, clean, and raise children are antiquated. The roles and responsibilities a couple will share in marriage ought not to be etched in stone by ancient traditions. Young adults, when meeting others, should discuss their expectations and assumptions regarding how their future partner will behave in a marriage. This may clarify these matters and help avoid potential marital challenges because of false or inaccurate assumptions and/or expectations. Young adults should recognize that their lives and marital relationships can and should be more balanced than those of their parents. Indian parents should also be mindful that fighting, anger, and disrespect in their own marriage and family may have a negative impact on how their children perceive the traditional Indian marriage

III

The New Indian Marriage

For thousands of Indian families, the arranged marriage system has worked well. The couples married under this system have tremendous faith in the decisions of their parents, and they make a firm commitment to one another. These couples learn to love each other after the wedding. This system, particularly if it is solely based on the factors discussed previously, such as caste, dowry, family status, and so forth, may not meet the needs of many young people today. Instead, a hybrid marriage format has been used increasingly, where parents prescreen young adults and introduce their children to potential partners. They then leave it completely up to the two individuals to determine whether or not to pursue a relationship. I would put my own marriage in this category. My parents introduced me to a few young men they had prescreened, but ultimately it was my decision whether to marry and whom to marry. More often today, young adults are electing to find their own partner after meeting people at school, work, or social events. This has long been referred to as a *love marriage* in India. Finally, there are several young adults who are choosing not to get married. They have full careers, fabulous friends, and a loving family. They do not perceive the need for a spouse or partner.

In the fall of 2012, Pew Research Center, in association with *Time Magazine*, conducted a nationwide poll exploring the modern marriage and posing questions about what people want and expect out of marriage and family life. What they found is that marriage in practical terms is just not as necessary as it used to be. Nearly 40 percent of people surveyed thought marriage was obsolete. Just as in India, women in the United States have rising earning power and do not need to stay in a marriage that makes them unhappy.

The decision as to whether to get married, and if so, the best process for getting married, is one that young adults must make, ideally in consultation with their parents and family and after much self-reflection. To have meaningful input in this decision, parents should have open, honest discussions with their children about marriage even when they are in their late teens and early twenties, as this is generally when young people become seriously interested in the opposite sex and in long-term relationships. Children should not feel shy, embarrassed, or scared to talk to their parents about these matters. Parents should respectfully, and in an open-minded manner, explore with their child the advantages and disadvantages of each option. Ideally, they should reach a consensus about the approach that best suits the needs and expectations of the child. Parents should keep in mind that what they want may not be exactly what their child wants, and that the ultimate goal is the child's happiness.

Assessing Compatibility

When a young person elects to find a life partner on his or her own, as opposed to taking the arranged marriage route, he or she bears greater responsibility for the success of the marriage. In arranged marriages, the couple can always blame their parents for forcing them into the union. In the case of love marriages, young people have to own their decisions. In order to feel confident about the decision of whether a person is an appropriate partner, it is helpful to explore compatibility, shared values, life goals, and expectations.

While some young men and women individually may be very nice people with great backgrounds and wonderful families, they may in fact be incompatible. One may enjoy outdoor activities, traveling, and socializing. The other may be more of an introvert and prefer to stay at home. One may enjoy eating meat dishes, and the other may be a vegetarian. One may have an interest in having several children, while the other does not care to have kids. She may wish to work, and he may want her to remain a housewife. One may enjoy shopping and eating out, and the other may be a penny pincher. One may believe it is the wife's job to take care of the home and kids, and the other may believe that these responsibilities should be shared. One may wish to live abroad, and one may wish to live in India. One may want his or her parents to reside with the couple, and one may want to have independence and privacy. These differences in perspective can be a continuing source of conflict, regardless of the fact that the husband and wife share a common culture and faith.

 It has traditionally been the expectation in Indian marriages that if there are differences in perspective, the woman will adjust her needs to be consistent with her husband's desires. This sacrifice of personal preferences and needs by women is no longer the norm. Women are increasingly expressing their views and making their expectations and desires known to their husbands. This is a tremendous shift in the modern Indian marriage. As a result, it is more important that young men and women enter into marriages with as much information as possible about each other to preclude surprises or unpleasant conflicts that could lead to dissolution of the marriage.

Questions to Assess Compatibility

In lieu of marriage brokers or middlemen, there are several types of questions that one may employ in trying to gain information to assess compatibility. Appropriately using questions during conversations can make a tremendous difference in the amount of information that is shared. An open-ended question is the most effective type of question to ask a person to invite the sharing of information. This allows the speaker to share what he or she feels is important, as opposed to limiting or narrowing the information that is shared. Open-ended questions are perfect to get to know someone and to engage in a positive dialogue. The following sections demonstrate the primary types of questions that can be used to gain information as a young Indian adult assesses compatibility of a potential partner.

Open-Ended Questions

These are broad questions that allow for a narrative answer. They are used to gain a great deal of information, to begin two-way communication, and to ask sensitive questions.

These are the very best type of question to ask when first meeting a person, as they allow open sharing of information that the speaker feels is important.

1. What are you looking for in a relationship?

2. What are your short-term goals in life?

3. What are your long-term goals in life?

4. If you had one day to live, what would you do and why?

5. How would you describe your ideal life partner?

6. What makes you happy?

7. How do you deal with difficult situations?

8. How do you like to relax?

Clarification Questions

These are questions that enable you to gain more specific information or to ensure understanding. The purpose of clarification questions is to encourage elaboration and to clear up confusing messages.

1. By saying you are religious, do you mean that you pray daily?

2. Are you saying that you don't enjoy cooking or that you don't know how to cook?

3. Are you a strict vegetarian, or do you eat eggs?

Closed Questions

These are specific and allow for only short answers, usually yes or no. They can be used to try to stop the speaker, to direct the conversation to a specific topic, or to gain control of the discussion. These questions may discourage productive discussion and result in getting less information.

1. Did you date anyone before we met?

2. Have you been in your current job long?

3. Have you been to India recently?

4. Were you born and raised in the United States?

Leading Questions

These are questions where the answer is implied. They are more likely to direct a particular response as opposed to eliciting more information.

1. You aren't from New York originally, are you?

2. You like watching Bollywood movies, don't you?

3. You don't eat meat, do you?

4. You understand Hindi, don't you?

Directive Questions

These are questions that obtain specific information, and they can be used in conjunction with other questions.

1. If you had to live with a non-vegetarian, could you do it?

2. Would you mind if I drank alcohol socially?

3. Would you be willing to visit my parents in India at least once a year with me?

4. Would you be open to sharing house work?

Reflective Questions

These are questions that encourage expansion of information by demonstrating listening. The responses to these questions lead to greater understanding.

1. It sounds like my inability to speak Hindi is really bothering you. Could you tell me more about that?

2. It appears that you have a real passion for the field of medicine but you are worried about the toll that residency training will have on our relationship. Help me better understand what concerns you.

3. I get the impression that you are worried about what role my parents will play in our life. Can you tell me more about your concerns?

Shaadi Remix

It is helpful to think about questions that illuminate the characteristics individuals find important in a future partner. The questions should enable a person to assess traits, including what is often referred to as the Big Five personality traits: extroversion, agreeableness, conscientiousness, emotional stability, and openness to experience.

Sample Questions to Elicit Useful Information When Contemplating Marriage

Education

1. What is your educational background?

2. Where did you go to school?

3. Do you plan on pursuing higher studies?

4. If you are planning on pursuing a higher education, what kind of time commitment does that involve?

5. How do you feel about your spouse seeking a higher education?

6. How do you see the best way of financing your spouse's education or your own or both?

Work

1. Do you have a job, and if so, what is it?

2. If you do not have a job now, do you plan on working?

3. What are your career goals?

4. What kind of time commitment does your work involve?

5. Does your work involve travel, or might it in the future?

6. How would you effectively balance work and life?

7. What does your work mean to you?

Family

1. Are you close to your family?

2. Do you visit them often?

3. Where do your family members live?

4. How often do you visit India?

5. Do you like to visit India? If not, why not?

6. Do you want children, and if so, how many?

7. What type of family environment did you grow up in?

8. How would you describe your communication with your parents?

9. How did your parents provide discipline?

10. What values did your parents emphasize?

11. How did your family deal with conflict?

12. Who made the decisions in your family?

13. Were your parents equal partners in their relationship?

14. Did you grow up in a loving and supportive environment?

15. What were your greatest challenges with your parents?

16. Were there any other people in your family who played important roles in your life?

17. What type of family life do you want?

18. How would you seek to raise your children?

19. What values would you seek to instill in your children?

20. What disciplinary methods do you think are appropriate?

21. Whose responsibility is it to raise children?

22. What does family mean to you?

Lifestyle and Money

1. What kind of lifestyle do you have?

2. What kind of lifestyle do you want to have?

3. What is your dream home? Dream car?

4. How important is money to you?

5. What are your financial goals?

6. When do you want to retire?

7. How would you describe your spending habits?

8. If you found $100, what would you do with it?

9. Do you enjoy shopping?

10. How do you think large item purchase decisions should be made?

11. What type of financial decision-making would you like to have in a marriage?

12. Do you think spouses should tell each other everything related to financial matters?

13. Should a couple keep their earnings in separate accounts?

14. Do you like receiving expensive gifts?

15. Do you enjoy celebrating birthdays, anniversaries, and other special occasions?

16. Do you like splurging on extravagances? If so, how often and what kind?

17. Do you like to take vacations, and if so, describe your ideal vacation?

18. Do you believe in saving for the future?

19. Where do you see yourself in ten years, in twenty years?

20. What does leading a successful life mean to you?

Household Matters

1. What is your perspective on whether household responsibilities should be shared?

2. Ideally, how would household responsibilities be shared?

3. What is your least favorite household chore?

4. What is your biggest pet peeve?

5. How do you organize your daily routine? Do you use lists or just go with the flow?

6. Are you a morning person or a night owl?

7. Do you prefer planning and research before making decisions, or do you prefer spontaneity?

8. Do you need down time or relaxation time every day, or are you always on the go?

9. How do you make important decisions?

10. What types of decisions do you think require consensus between partners?

11. What decisions would you prefer to make independently?

12. Do you enjoy cooking? If so, what items?

13. Do you enjoy eating out? If so, how often?

14. Did you have a house-cleaner growing up?

15. Are you comfortable with a messy house, or are you a neat freak?

16. Do you pick up after yourself, or have you always had someone to do it for you?

17. What do you do when you get angry?

18. How do you like to deal with conflict?

Extracurricular Activities

1. What are your hobbies?

2. Do you like an active social life?

3. Do you drink?

4. Do you enjoy evenings out or evenings at home?

5. What do you like to do to relax on weekends?

6. Do you enjoy the outdoors?

7. Can you swim?

8. Do you like adventurous activities?

9. Do you enjoy watching movies?

10. Do you like Indian movies?

11. What type of music do you enjoy listening to?

12. Do you exercise regularly?

13. What makes you laugh?

14. What makes you happy?

15. Do you like to have time for yourself?

16. Do you enjoy reading?

17. Are you a fan of the arts, theater, or dance?

18. Do you prefer doing things in large groups or with your partner?

Hinduism/Culture

1. Are you a Hindu?

2. Describe how you practice your faith.

3. Do you have a prayer room in your home?

4. How often do you pray?

5. Who is your favorite god or house god?

6. Do you celebrate important Hindu festivals?

7. How often do you visit the temple?

8. Do you observe fasts occasionally?

9. Are you a vegetarian?

10. Does it bother you if others eat meat in your presence?

11. Do you wear or feel comfortable wearing Indian ethnic clothes?

12. Do you have Indian friends?

13. Are you embarrassed when you see Indians in public wearing ethnic clothes or speaking in their native tongue?

14. Do you speak your native language?

15. What customs do you observe from your Indian community?

16. Do you enjoy Indian food?

17. What are your most important values?

18. How involved are your parents in your life?

19. How do you identify yourself: as an Indian, American, or both?

20. What challenges, if any, did you face growing up as an Indian?

21. Is it important to you that the Indian culture and the Hindu faith are passed down to your children?

By gaining more information in a neutral and candid manner when a couple has gone beyond mere physical attraction, it becomes easier to determine whether there is compatibility and the potential for a successful marriage. Some couples move beyond just dating to living together to assess compatibility. According to Pew Research, in the United States, there was a 13 percent increase in couples living together from 2009 to 2010. This has been attributed to the recession. Unfortunately, couples who move in together before they get married don't divorce any less often. In the Indian community, while cohabitation before marriage is rare, it is happening more often, particularly when couples seriously anticipate getting married. The decision to cohabit is one that young adults have to make responsibly, and ideally in consultation with their family, especially as it conflicts with core Hindu values.

IV

Effective
Communication
in Marriage

AS DISCUSSED EARLIER, THE INDIAN MARRIAGES THAT ARE not successful are often unions that are formalized based on factors that parents identify as significant—such as caste, family status, horoscope, and so forth—with little or no input from the young couple. Additional factors common to the Indian marriages that fail include unmet expectations, lack of respect, and/or different perspectives on gender roles and responsibilities. These challenges impact both arranged and love marriages. These differences can generally be worked out through effective communication and conflict resolution skills. Unfortunately, many young couples do not invest the energy and time in effectively communicating or nurturing their relationship, and are more likely to end a relationship when they feel unhappy. Whether a marriage is arranged or the result of dating/co-habiting, it is critical that couples address and attempt to resolve issues in their marriage. The following are communication and problem-solving skills that may be helpful to couples experiencing conflict.

Conflict

Conflict in relationships is natural. When we think of conflict, negative images immediately come to mind: anger, frustration, fighting, disagreement, stress, and anxiety. High conflict causes a strong emotional and physical response in all of us. We often can't sleep or eat when we are in conflict. We feel burdened and weighed down by the stress of the conflict. The relationship affected by the conflict is strained and weakened. The reason we have such a strong reaction is that when we are in conflict, our brain perceives the conflict as a threat. As human beings, we all have five basic human needs:

- **Security** – The sense that something we value will not be taken away from us for no good reason.

- **Respect** – The sense of being valued and acknowledged for who we are and for our contributions.

- **Fairness** – The sense that we are being treated equitably and judged using objective criteria.

- **Autonomy** – The sense that we are independent and have some control over our lives.

- **Belonging** – The sense that we are part of something bigger than ourselves, such as a community or family.

When any one of these basic human needs is affected, our brain perceives it as a threat, and the amygdala, the prehistoric part of the brain, is triggered. There is an immediate secretion of hormones, including adrenaline, in our body, and we automatically choose one of two paths: fight or flight.

In a marital conflict, we often perceive a threat to one or more of these basic human needs. For example, an argument over how much money one spouse spent on clothes or jewelry may lead to the perceived threat of a need for financial security and autonomy. A conflict regarding the time a spouse returns from work may be perceived as a threat to respect and autonomy. A fight over comments made by the in-laws may impact the need for respect and belonging. An argument over household chores and responsibilities impacts the need for fairness. The decision to fight or flee in the midst of conflict is the easiest and most natural choice, but these are not the best ways to address a conflict. Because preservation of the relationship is so important in marital conflicts, the better approach is to engage in respectful communication to reach a collaborative resolution.

Active Listening

The key to all successful relationships is effective communication. Effective communication creates a positive environment and facilitates the development of trust and rapport. These are essential ingredients for a strong marital relationship. The first thing to break down when a couple is in conflict is their communication. When I meet couples in the midst of a separation or divorce, they often cannot bear to look at each other, much less speak to each other. When they do speak, their words drip with hatred, anger, disappointment, mistrust, and frustration. They know each other's hot buttons and push them as hard as they can, intentionally seeking to inflict pain. Who ever said that words don't hurt? In the book *Blink*, Malcolm Gladwell shares the research of Dr. John Gottman, renowned psychologist, author, and expert on divorce prediction and marital stability, noting that a key predictor of marital discord is the use of language patterns that demonstrate contempt. Understanding how to engage in effective communication with a partner will help prevent misunderstandings, ensure that each partner is truly hearing and understanding the needs and interests of the other, and avoid the unnecessary escalation of conflict.

Professor Albert Mehrabian, professor emeritus in psychology at UCLA did research on verbal and non-verbal communication. He found that there are three elements to basic communication: words, tone, and body language. We often assume that words compromise the greatest part of communication, but in fact, Dr. Mehrabian's research shows that words make up only

7 percent of the message. The tone of voice—how loud or how soft and how fast or slow one speaks—comprises 38 percent of the message. Body language, which includes facial expressions, eye contact, posture, and gestures, comprises 55 percent of the message. Thus, over 90 percent of communication is non-verbal. Professor Mehrabian's research also shows that the message must be congruent in all three aspects. For example, if one were to yell loudly, "I don't have a problem with you!" that would not convey to the receiver that things are okay. The tone would overpower the words, and the receiver would believe that, in fact, there is a problem. Such research is valuable, teaching us that when communicating with someone, such as our partner, *how* we say something is more important than *what* we say.

A key aspect of communication is active listening. We spend over 70 percent of the day communicating. Of that time, we spend approximately 35 percent of the time speaking and 40 percent of the time listening. The sad fact is that we listen only at about 25 percent of our potential. This means that we ignore, forget, distort, or misunderstand 75 percent of what we hear. We listen best when there is a penalty or a payoff. All couples should recognize that, in marriage, the payoff of good listening is a happy spouse. This should be incentive enough to work on effective listening skills.

Active listening is basically:

- Listening to hear, not to answer

- Understanding the meaning behind the words

- Hearing the emotional content of the communications

- Using skilled feedback to let the person know his or her message was received.

When a spouse is speaking, the other spouse who is receiving the information must strive to focus 100 percent on what is being said. Listening with full attention is difficult because we have many distractions in our world—the phone, TV, work, our children, and other things. When one is not actively listening to a spouse, it is clearly apparent, as poor listening is characterized by lack of eye contact, the inability to respond to questions related to the information that is being shared, and body language that suggests indifference. A spouse knows immediately when he or she is not being heard and takes the lack of listening as an indication of disrespect and lack of caring.

Active listening requires a great deal of concentration and effort. It entails full and complete attention to the speaker. It is truly being present, both mentally and physically, with the speaker. To actively listen, one must do the following:

- Take a moment to relax and clear your mind of any and all distractions, assumptions, and preconceived ideas.

- Concentrate on the words, tone, and body language of the speaker.

- Demonstrate interest by using eye contact, leaning forward, nodding to show acknowledgement of receipt of the message.

- Empathize by summarizing your understanding of the speaker's statements.

- Don't try to "figure out" the situation—or its solution—too early.

- Learn to be comfortable with silence.

- Learn to be comfortable with a certain level of emotion—as long as it is helping you or the other person learn or understand.

A good listener will not finish the speaker's sentences and assume that he or she knows what is going to be said. A good listener does not rehearse or plan a response while the other person is still speaking. A good listener will not allow his or her mind to wander to other matters. A good listener will not focus attention on criticizing the speaker as opposed to hearing the speaker. A good listener will not fake attention to the speaker. A good listener will not interrupt the speaker. A good listener will not tune out a speaker because he or she disagrees with them.

If one can practice good listening skills, the next step of effective communication is understanding the meaning behind the words and body language. As Steven Covey says in his book *The Seven Habits of Highly Successful People*, we must first seek to understand before we seek to be understood. We must try to gain a greater appreciation of the concerns being expressed by our spouse and convey that we understand his or her perspective. It is only then that our spouse will actively listen to our concerns and perspective. There are several communication techniques that can be used to demonstrate understanding.

Communication Techniques to Support Understanding

Some communication skills that couples in conflict can employ to improve understanding are:

Paraphrasing

In paraphrasing we combine the facts (content of the message) and the feelings into one statement. The purpose is to focus on the content of the message and highlight particular feelings and issues. This helps the speaker know he or she was heard and understood.

I understand you are very angry at me because I am not assisting you with household chores. You are exhausted after taking care of the kids all day and would appreciate it if I would help with the dishes or giving the children a bath so that you can have some down time too.

Summarizing

Summarizing involves pulling together in condensed form what another has said. It is different from paraphrasing in that it deals with more information at once. The purpose is to tie together elements of messages and identify common themes.

I understand the past year has been very difficult for you since my parents have come to live with us. You do not mean them any disrespect, and you recognize that they are here because they need help because of health reasons. However, you are frustrated by our lack of privacy and your loss of freedom. You are tired of having to cook fresh Indian meals twice a day. You miss ordering out for pizza and just relaxing in front of the TV. You can't tell them to keep their room clean and you feel like you are serving them hand and foot from morning to night. You feel like they are always watching you and criticizing everything you do. You don't know how much longer you can take this, and you are worried about the impact it is having on our relationship.

Reframing

People will often use negative and highly charged language when speaking to one another. Restating the concern or interest being expressed by a person in a more neutral and future-focused manner enables constructive conversation. It is often the case that underneath very angry language, there is actually a need being expressed. Behind every complaint, there is a request.

Effective Communication in Marriage

Reframing language seeks to pull out from the toxic language a more neutral understanding of what is being requested.

Reframing Examples:

- "You are such a lazy person! You see me working all day, and you don't even lift a finger to help."

This can be reframed as:

> *I believe that it is important that we share equally in the household chores. We both work hard to provide for our family and are tired at the end of the day. If we can find a way to share these responsibilities, they will be accomplished faster and better so we can both have time to relax.*

- "You are never around when I need you! I have to do everything myself, and I am tired of it."

This can be reframed as:

> *I miss you and I need you to be there for me and our family. I enjoy doing things with you and feel awkward and alone when I am the only one at parties without my spouse. You are missing out on all the key events in our children's lives. They always ask where you are, and I have to make excuses. I want you to be more present and involved in the future.*

- "You never listen to me. I told you several times not to loan money to your family, but you did anyway, and now we are never going to get it back. You don't care about me or our own family's problems."

This can an be reframed as:

I understand that you love your brother and care about his well-being. I want you to hear my concern that if you continue loaning money to him, he will come to depend on it, and we may not have sufficient funds for our expenses. Especially given that your brother has been unemployed for the past three years, it is clear that he is not in a position to pay back these loans any time soon. We are also at a critical stage in our own family. One child is about to start college, and the other one needs a car. We have to balance our personal financial needs with those of our loved ones. As opposed to loaning him money, can you suggest that he get financial aid and go back to school to further his education?

Emotional Acknowledgment and Validation

These statements ensure that the feelings the other person is expressing are understood and acknowledged. Validating and respecting a person's feelings may help remove emotional blocks that are preventing good communication. The purpose is not necessarily to agree with the person but to convey listening and concern.

Examples of emotional acknowledgement:

I understand that you are angry that I bought a new pair of shoes. I know you feel like I am a spendthrift and don't care about our budget. It hurts you when I seem to disregard what we have discussed about our monthly expenses.

I know that you feel hurt each time my mother talks about how beautiful the girl she had wanted me to marry is or how bad your cooking is. I understand that it makes you feel inadequate and unappreciated. I recognize that you resent being compared to someone else and want to be valued and loved for who you are and for the special talents that you have.

In addition to the skills mentioned, there are some methods of communication that clearly do not support understanding.

Examples of Ineffective Communication

There are several examples of ineffective communication that Indian couples use and may not recognize as harmful.

Arguing

Disagreeing with a person or being defensive and trying to justify yourself creates the negative perception that you are thinking against the party with whom you are arguing.

> *You don't know how to treat your children. You scold them and spank them for no good reason. They secretly hate you and are scared of you! Don't ever come near my kids.*

> *You are the one spoiling our children. You let them watch TV whenever they want to. They go to bed late and eat junk food. You buy them things they don't need just because they ask for it. I am trying to instill some discipline in them before it is too late!*

Minimizing

Minimizing is dismissing the message or the feelings of the spouse. This conveys a negative and belittling approach.

> *So what if I enjoy collecting* Playboy *magazines. I can't help that there are beautiful naked women in them. They are like exotic cars. You can't help but notice them. You should not take it personally. All men enjoy seeing attractive women. It's not a big deal.*

Using Negative Words

Using words such as *never* and *always* is unhelpful to constructive conversations. Avoid using words that point to negative behavior.

> *You are always in a bad mood and never want to have any fun. All you want to do is work, work, and work! You won't even go out to dinner with me. You always say, "It's too expensive. Let's just eat at home." I am sick and tired of it.*

Giving Advice

This involves telling the person what he or she should or should not do. This is dis-empowering language, which attempts to substitute for the person's authority over the matter and is perceived as thinking for the other person.

> *I think you should stop hanging around those friends from work. You are never home anymore. All you want to do is spend time with them, and you are neglecting everything else. Just because they decide to take a trip to Vegas this weekend doesn't mean that you have to join them!*

Skills for Assertive Communication

Another key aspect of communication is learning how to share information in a way that makes it easy for the other person to hear it and understand you, without getting defensive. This is an important skill for Indian women in particular, as they are not generally comfortable asserting their perspective and so often go unheard.

Skill #1 – "I" vs. "You" Language

Using the pronoun *I* at the beginning of a statement helps one to take responsibility for his or her perspective. It promotes cooperation and understanding when making statements to others. This is in contrast to "you" statements, which promote an atmosphere of conflict by sounding accusatory, judgmental, and even threatening to others. "You" statements tend to elicit a defensive or negative response. Communicate respectfully, not aggressively. Express your thoughts, feelings, and opinions positively and directly, in an honest, open, straightforward, and sincere manner. Aggressive communication causes anger and humiliation. "I" statements can make the difference between getting cooperation or resistance when disagreeing with a spouse.

Examples:

I feel hurt when you walk away from me when I am talking to you.

I am scared when you don't call me to let me know that you are coming home late.

Skill # 2 – Expectation Statements

The ability to anticipate your spouse's statements, objections, or concerns is a means of establishing rapport and understanding. The goal in an expectation statement is to anticipate your spouse's reactions and incorporate these reactions into your statements. This will likely produce a positive outcome, gain acceptance for what you want, and avoid conflict. When making a request of your spouse or when responding to your spouse, ask yourself what reactions or objections he or she might have. Then incorporate the anticipated reaction or objection into your statement.

Examples:

To Gain Cooperation

- You – *Would you mind helping me in the garden?*

- Spouse – *Sorry, but I am very busy today.*

Shaadi Remix

Expectation Statement

- You – *I know you are very busy finishing your report. I really need your help with the garden before it starts to rain.*

- Spouse – *Okay. I can only spare an hour because of my deadline.*

To Influence

- You – *I would like to go back to work again.*

- Spouse – *I don't think so. The last time you got a job you went crazy because you couldn't handle the stress of the baby, home, and your work.*

Expectation Statement

- You – *I know that the last time I went back to work it was really hard for me to balance everything. I found a part-time job opportunity that I think will give me enough flexibility to take care of the baby and home, and also get out of the house each day. I would like to try working again.*

- Spouse – *Okay. I know it is hard staying at home all day without any adult company. Why don't you try it and see how it goes."*

To Gain Respect

- Spouse – *Hey, honey, would you get me a cup of tea?*

- You – *Okay.*

Expectation Statement

- Spouse – *Hey, honey, would you get me a cup of tea?*

- You – *I know that you don't mean to take advantage of me, and I enjoy making you tea, but I think it would be nice if once in a while you would bring me a cup of tea or get it yourself when you see that I am busy doing something else. I would really appreciate that.*

To Overcome Stereotypes

- You – *I have an idea that might work with our budgetary problem.*

- Spouse – *I don't think you understand. This issue is very complicated.*

Expectation Statement

- You – *I know I do not have a business degree, but I have an idea that I think may work in this situation. Please hear me out.*

- Spouse – *All right. Tell me your suggestion.*

Skill #3 – Mutual Interest Statements

We are often motivated to cooperate if something will further our needs and interests. As human beings we have self-interests, such as money, power, status, recognition, and security.

At times, we can inspire cooperation and understanding if we can appeal to mutual interests. You must first determine your spouse's areas of interest and incorporate them into your statement.

Example:

Statement by Wife: *I know that as responsible parents, we need to drop our children off at school before we go to work. At the same time, punctuality at work is key to our productivity and meeting our bosses' expectations. What ideas do you have to ensure that we are both able to get to work on time, and also get the kids to school?*

Statement by Husband: *I know that you have been working very hard to get your graduate degree and it will ultimately enable you to get a better job. I recognize that you do not have time to cook and clean. I also know that we both care about the children, their activities and homework, as well as the upkeep of our home. What ideas do you have to ensure that you have enough time to study and achieve your goal of graduating this year, as well keeping up with the kids and the house?*

Skill #4 – Meta Communication

Meta-communication is a person's non-verbal communication of feelings, emotions, or attitudes that may not be directly expressed. At a meta-level, a spouse would comment to his or her partner about the underlying feelings the spouse has observed. To engage in meta-communication, one must actively listen to the other for the unspoken part of the message by focusing on the tone and body language. A spouse must use his or her intuition to check whether there are feelings, attitudes, or emotions not being expressed. Often a spouse can sense anger, frustration, hurt, sadness, fear, or other emotions. A meta-communication statement should acknowledge the spouse's feelings.

The following are examples of phrases for responding to meta-level emotions that are blocking communication:

* *From the tone of your voice, it sounds like you are feeling disappointed.*

- *I get the feeling that you're upset about something. Can we talk about it?*

- *From the look in your eyes, I have a sense that you're confused.*

- *Your facial expressions suggest you're feeling hurt. Is that right?*

- *I've noticed you not looking at me directly. Are you preoccupied with something else or worried about something?*

Themes in Unsuccessful Marriages

In mediating divorce and separation matters for Indian couples, there are some issues that arise quite often, largely because of traditional gender roles and cultural expectations. Indian couples that are experiencing conflict around these issues must communicate openly and respectfully about these matters.

Shared responsibilities

Marriage is a partnership. In most families, both the husband and wife work. Where the wife does not work outside the home, she is often caring for the children and is responsible for other household duties. The wife does not necessarily have to be the one to do all the cooking, cleaning, and child rearing. In an era when both spouses are usually well educated and work, spouses must discuss and negotiate how responsibilities are to be shared. It might be that if a couple can afford it, hiring a house cleaner once a month or biweekly is a great investment. Selecting a nanny to assist with child care is also helpful. This enables both individuals the opportunity to relax or do more enjoyable activities during the precious time they have away from work and with each other.

Shared Expenses

One of the biggest conflicts between couples has to do with finances. Women often expect men to pay the rent or mortgage, all the utilities, and other necessary large expenses. Women often assume that their income is intended for their pleasure and spend it on their hair, make-up, clothing, jewelry, and other personal items. It might be that this arrangement works great, but couples need to discuss this. They need to clarify how necessities, food, shelter, taxes, gas, car payments, and other expenses will be paid for. Ideally, if both spouses work, this is a shared responsibility. A budget for fun or luxury items should be developed and enjoyed by both.

All too often one spouse, often the husband, resents that he bears the burden of all household expenses, food costs, child care/education expenses, and health care expenses. The chances for conflicts over money to erupt are greater when couples do not take the time to review their assets, liabilities, finances, and monthly expenses. I have seen spouses take money out of each other's accounts without prior discussion, or refuse to pay for household necessities. This behavior is dangerous, as it can impact credit ratings, risk the couple losing their lease or defaulting on a loan, or even losing a space in a coveted child care facility.

Respect

Respect is a basic principle in all successful marital relationships. If a couple does not hold each other in high regard and treat each with appreciation and honor, it can be very detrimental to a marriage. A couple can lose respect for each other in many ways. As discussed earlier, the manner and nature of communications between a couple can convey respect. When people do not actively listen to the concerns their spouses express, their spouses will believe they do not care about their perspective or feelings. Over time resentment can build up. Communication that is harsh or angry elicits the same type of response. Use of profanity or derogatory terms when addressing one's spouse is very hard to recover from. When couples begin making statements that extend to their parents or family, it is akin to taking a knife to their heart. Personal attacks and disregard for each other's feelings and needs is humiliating and devastating. A couple can agree to disagree about an issue without being disrespectful to each other. Silence and lack of communication over an extended period can also lead to anger and misunderstanding.

Another point to recognize is that we judge ourselves by our intentions and others by their behaviors. It may be that we know in our mind why we do or say certain things and feel perfectly justified doing so. Our spouse, however, can only draw conclusions based on what he or she sees. Our spouse cannot read our mind. As a result, if our spouse sees conduct that appears rude, unappreciative, or hurtful, they will draw the conclusion that there is no respect in the relationship. Open and respectful communication about our intentions can help prevent spouses from reaching inaccurate or harmful conclusions.

Mina works very hard to prepare a delicious dinner for Karan. Karan comes home very late from work and does not call Mina to tell her he is coming late. He does not eat and goes straight to bed. Mina is furious and does not sleep well all night. She is seething the next morning when Karan comes downstairs. He looks at her angry face and, without a word, heads out the door for work.

Mina's assumption is that Karan is cruel and uncaring because of his lack of attention to her and her efforts in preparing him a

---

wonderful dinner. This is not the first time he has done this. She feels unappreciated and disrespected. Karan is dealing with a very important deadline at work. His boss is very demanding and his job is at stake. He did not have a moment to call Mina yesterday to tell her he would be late because he was on a lengthy overseas conference call. He was exhausted when he came home and just needed to sleep five hours so he could function the next day for his big presentation. He does not understand why Mina is so moody and angry all the time, but he does not have the energy to discuss it. He wishes she would understand and respect him for how hard he works.

If Mina and Karan don't take the time to discuss their concerns, their marriage could be in serious trouble. The time they should invest in communication and clarifying concerns and expectations would be well spent.

Anger

Couples should not discuss things when they are angry. It is normal to get upset. Couples who never fight are not the norm. Emotions are natural and demonstrate that you care about the person or the issue at hand. When we get angry, the blood flows away from the rational part of the brain, the frontal cortex, to the amygdala, which controls our fight-or-flight responses. As a result, it is very difficult to make decisions or engage in thoughtful discussions when we are upset. There is an inverse relationship between high emotion and the ability to problem solve. When couples are angry or arguing, they should not try to resolve important issues. It is best to just walk away, calm down, and then clarify matters when they can speak more respectfully.

Trust

Stephen Covey in his book *The Speed of Trust* says, "There is one thing that is common to every individual, relationship, team, family, organization, nation, economy, and civilization through the world – one thing which, if removed, will destroy the most powerful government, the most successful business, the most thriving economy, the most influential leadership, the greatest friendship, the strongest character, the deepest love. On the other hand, if developed and leveraged, that one thing has the potential to create unparalleled success and prosperity in every dimension of life. That one thing is trust."

The ability to believe in and count on the word and integrity of a spouse is vital to a successful relationship. Once trust is compromised, it is incredibly hard to reestablish. Successful couples engage in behavior that exemplifies that they are trustworthy. They speak honestly and admit to mistakes. They are consistent and reliable. They accept responsibility and follow through on promises. Trust is a precious core value in marriage and must be nurtured every day. When a partner engages in behavior that compromises trust, the concerns should be discussed at the earliest possible time so that mistrust does not continue to grow.

V

Effective Conflict Resolution in Marriage

A LL COUPLES WILL AT SOME POINT IN THEIR RELATIONSHIP have conflict. The most important thing is how they manage and work through that conflict. The first thing to be prepared for is how to deal with strong emotions.

Dealing with Anger

Partners in conflict have strong emotions, which can prevent them from solving their problems. Anger comes from a sense that a basic human need is at risk. It stems from fear, powerlessness, or loss of control. Healthy anger provides energy for positive change. Unhealthy anger, however, is destructive. When emotions become too strong, a couple cannot solve problems using a reasonable process. There is an inverse relationship between anger and the ability to problem solve. The greater the anger, the less one can think clearly. The two times that are best for constructive problem solving are before emotions escalate or after they have de-escalated. To most appropriately deal with anger expressed by a spouse, one can do the following:

- Know and understand your own response to anger, your defensiveness and hot buttons.

» Remain calm when the other person is mad and listen actively.

» Use silence.

- Name the emotion: "I hear your anger. It is all right that you are angry."

  » Ask your spouse directly for his or her thoughts, feelings, and opinions.

  » Acknowledge your spouse's feelings.

  » Summarize your spouse's point of view in neutral terms.

  » Identify issues objectively.

- Create a safe place to vent away from the children, the public, or other distractions. Allow the angry spouse to express and talk through feelings and emotions.

- Avoid personal attacks and focus on the problem.

  » Concentrate on understanding what your spouse is saying.

  » Listen for both facts and feelings.

  » If your spouse says you do not understand, communicate that it is important to you that you do.

  » If you disagree, remember that it's still important to validate your spouse's feelings.

  » Pay attention to nonverbal cues and body language.

- Take a break if needed. Allow time to think and regroup.

  » Ask if your spouse wishes to continue the discussion at this time or take some time apart to think.

  » Determine whether you are emotionally capable

of dealing with the situation or need some time to process.

- Consider the source; identify why your spouse may be angry. Try to address the causes, not the behavior.

  » Use positive language.

  » Use statements that will help your spouse focus on the future.

  » Steer away from blaming each other.

Anger is a normal emotion. The key is to manage it in a way that is productive.

Strategies for Dealing with Conflict

When an individual is in conflict, he or she has a tendency to react in a particular manner. Conflict-resolution specialists are familiar with the instrument called the Thomas-Kilmann Conflict Mode Instrument, which was developed to help people determine their approach to conflict. The answers to the survey questions may vary depending on the context of the conflict or the person the conflict is with, but the survey gives people a sense of their predisposition or approach to conflict. Thomas Kilmann identifies five primary strategies for dealing with conflict (Thomas-Kilmann 8).

Avoidance – Conflict? What Conflict?

This strategy involves denying or ignoring a conflict in the hopes that it will disappear. The tendency of a spouse using this technique is to withdraw or become silent when there is a conflict. This approach is often appropriate when the issue is trivial or a decision is not necessary. For example, if a spouse forgets to hang his coat up one evening, that is something that can be overlooked. The issue is not a big deal, because it is easy enough to hang up the coat yourself. On the other hand, if a spouse routinely leaves clothes, shoes, or other personal items lying around the house, that can become quite bothersome and lead to feelings of resentment for having to pick up after the spouse constantly. The avoidance approach is inappropriate when negative feelings may linger or one really cares about the issues. If avoidance is used habitually, then issues will never get resolved and anger could begin to build. It is not unusual for Indian couples to avoid conflict in the interest of maintaining harmony.

Accommodation – Whatever you want is okay with me.

In the accommodation strategy, one agrees with or is willing to appease the partner. This approach is often appropriate when the issue is not important to you, you realize you are wrong, or you believe in taking turns on an issue. For example, if you and your spouse are deciding on a place to go for dinner, one of you might want Chinese food and the other Italian. If the relationship is more important to you than what food you eat, you would be likely to choose your spouse's favorite restaurant. The challenge comes when your spouse always insists on eating Chinese and never entertains the idea of trying what you like. The accommodation approach is typically the predisposition of women, particularly Indian women, because they care about preserving the relationship, giving deference to their spouse, and putting their needs last. This approach is inappropriate when one grows to resent being taken advantage of and feels that his or her acquiescence is misused habitually. If one accommodates constantly, it is highly likely that he or she will explode one day when compliance becomes too great a task.

Competition – My way or the highway.

The competition strategy involves trying to compete, control, coerce, or fight. This approach is appropriate when an emergency looms and a decision has to be made, or when others don't really care what happens. This style is often inappropriate when cooperation from others is important. The competitive approach causes a shift in the balance of power in a marital relationship. It suggests that the stronger spouse, often the husband, has the authority to make all the decisions. Little attention is paid to the feelings and interests of the partner. The partner's self-respect is diminished needlessly. The married couple does not work together as a team. The less powerful partner basically gives up in conflict situations and feels devalued.

Compromise – Let's split the difference.

The compromise strategy involves some amount of bargaining, with a little something for everyone. This approach is appropriate when finding some solution is better than a stalemate. Here cooperation is important. For example, if a couple needs to buy a new vehicle for their growing family, the wife may desire a minivan. It is spacious and offers good safety features. The husband may worry about the look of the vehicle and want four-wheel drive, as they live in an area with bad winter weather. The couple may compromise and decide to buy an SUV with room for seven passengers, a large trunk, and all-wheel drive. The compromise approach is inappropriate when you can't live with the consequences of the compromise.

Collaboration – How can we solve this problem together?

The collaboration strategy seeks to gather information, look for shared interests, consider alternatives, engage in dialogue, and develop creative solutions. This approach is appropriate when the issues and relationship are significant, cooperation is important, and there is hope to address everyone's concerns. This is the ideal way that couples should engage in problem solving any conflict. To take a simple example, if a family is planning a vacation and Mom wants to relax on the beach and have access to a spa, Dad wants to play golf, and the children want to go to an amusement park, a collaborative solution might be to visit Florida. This would enable each member of the family to respect one another's wishes and also enjoy what they want in a vacation destination. Collaborative problem solving requires time and patience. The couple must clearly communicate their needs and interests with each other.

In order to develop creative solutions in collaborative problem solving, it is helpful to understand the distinction between positions and interests (Fisher and Ury 40). When most of us speak, we express our desires in the form of positions or expectations. For example, if a spouse says, "I want dinner to be served at 7:30 PM," it sounds like a demand. The interest behind that demand is the reason *why* the spouse wants dinner to be served at 7:30. The reason or interest could be that the spouse gets indigestion if he goes to sleep too soon after eating. It could be that his favorite TV shows begin at 8:00. It could be that if he eats earlier, he gets hungry again later. It is helpful to understand the reason behind why a person expresses a position, as that allows one to identify multiple solutions to meet that need. When couples strive to work through conflict, it is critical that they listen carefully for the interest or need being expressed behind their demand. A simple question—"Help me understand why you want that" or "What is important to you about this?"—can clarify a great deal and enable spouses to discuss creatively an array of ideas for dealing with the conflict.

VI

Ending the Marriage

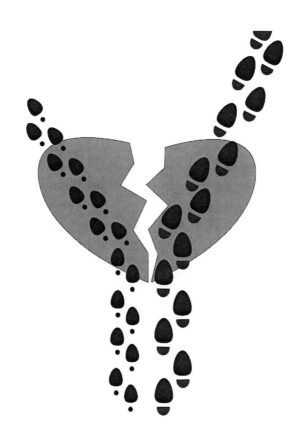

Reasons for Divorce

Regrettably, some Indian marriages, whether arranged or love unions, are not successful. Efforts at improving communication or engaging in collaborative problem solving fail, even with the assistance of parents or professional counselors. Some primary reasons Indian marriages fail include:

Drugs and Alcohol

One spouse's abusive drinking habits can make life very hard for the other spouse and every member of the family. This applies to any addictive substance, whether it is cocaine or prescribed painkillers. If one truly loves—or loved—his or her spouse, then he or she should try to help with the substance-abuse problem. But, a person can only suffer for so long. An addict or drug abuser has to want to change. If one does not see that desire, there is not much hope. There are unfortunately examples of Indian families where loss of a job led to substance and alcohol abuse, which in turn led to suicide and even murder-suicide.

Physical Abuse

Anyone involved in a physically abusive relationship should not hesitate to terminate the marriage. No spouse deserves physical abuse. Physical abuse is also usually accompanied by emotional abuse and verbal assaults, leading the abused spouse into a sort of paralysis, questioning if he or she is to blame. It is best not to get trapped in the cycle of violence. The sooner the relationship is ended safely, the sooner one can start enjoying life again and being treated with respect and dignity. Indian women who need assistance can contact SAWERA – South Asian Women's Empowerment and Resource Alliance at 503-778-7386 or go to their website sawera.org. SAWERA provides advocacy, empowerment and solidarity in a safe environment.

First, and perhaps most importantly, SAWERA provides **translation**. They are able to communicate in the client's native language.

They also assist in the following manner:

- Advocate for clients and support them in self-advocacy

- Provide culturally sensitive emotional support

- Provide referral for legal and immigration issues

- Help clients understand American cultural/legal system and customs

- Provide safety planning and risk assessment

- Provide emergency assistance

- Provide referrals for housing, counseling, medical care, food, clothing education, employment

- Provide transportation and other necessary services

- Provide co-case management with other agencies serving South Asian victims of domestic violence

Women can also contact the Asian Pacific Women's Center, www.apwcla.org or 800-799-7233, which is dedicated to providing a safe haven and support services for women and children who are survivors of domestic violence. Their mission is to provide an environment that is sensitive to the cultural and language needs of Asian and Pacific Islander survivors as they acquire the necessary skills and personal strength for self-sufficiency. Many localities, such as Chicago and Washington, D.C., have a regional domestic violence organization dedicated to supporting the needs of south Asian women who are victims of domestic violence.

Infidelity/Adultery

A spouse who feels it is necessary to find love on the side has completely abused the trust of his or her spouse. Infidelity should not be taken lightly and is often well-justified grounds for divorce. Culturally, it may be deemed acceptable for a man to have an affair or relationships with women while he is married, but that dishonors his wife and his marriage vows. Adultery is grounds for divorce under most fault-based divorce laws. It is unrealistic for a spouse to believe that adultery will have no impact on the marriage. Spouses should not be put in a position of having to tolerate infidelity. Instead, they have to decide whether the causes that led to the infidelity can be overcome and whether they wish to reestablish trust in the relationship with the unfaithful spouse. There are increasing numbers of Indian marriages ending due to adultery committed by either the husband or the wife. Ideally, before a spouse seeks love, attention, or support from another person, it is important that they communicate their feelings to their spouse, seek marriage counseling, and/ or the guidance of parents and loved ones.

Verbal/Mental Abuse

Insults can be every bit as debilitating as physical abuse. No one deserves to be put down or ridiculed for a flaw or inability to meet expectations. As a spouse, one is entitled to dignity and self-respect. Divorce may be the only avenue for recovering self-worth for someone who has been subjected to verbal and mental abuse.

Financial Disagreements

Finances are a major reason why some marriages fail—primarily spending habits. In strong marriages the couple is on the same page when it comes to money matters, and budgets are clearly defined and understood. This does not mean that both spouses should get full access to the savings account at all times, it just means that both spouses understand whatever system is in place. Perhaps one spouse has a personal savings account for spur-of-the-moment purchases. In and of itself, that is okay. However, tempers can flare when suddenly ten thousand dollars goes missing from the joint checking account, and one spouse was saving the money for the children's education or a new home. Repeated disagreements related to a spouse's spending habits, excessive fiscal control by one spouse, or financial mismanagement often lead to divorce.

Excessive Involvement of In-laws

In many Indian marriages, the in-laws play a very large role. Their excessive involvement or interference in personal affairs can strain a marriage. If one feels that the in-laws infringe upon his or her right to independence, respect, dignity, and self-worth, then this could contribute to the need for a divorce. Ideally, parents should be made aware of the impact their involvement is having on the marriage and they should be given an opportunity to limit or adjust their role to enable the couple to thrive.

When it is clear that there is lack of compatibility, respect, and trust, many Indian couples find it is best not to continue the relationship in order to save face in the community. If after two years of a relationship communication continues to be strained, conflicts arise daily, and emotions run at a feverish pitch, then it is unlikely the situation will improve. Couples often blame themselves or each other. Trying to remain together for the sake of society or for the children is a disservice to the entire family. The reality is that most Indian communities today are far more accepting of divorce. There may be rumors and gossip for a few days, but society does not have to deal with the issues that the couple faces on a daily basis. The people who are hurt when a marriage is in trouble are the couple and any children. The needs of the family, not the community, should be the first priority in making a decision about divorce.

Many Indian women tend to take advantage of the negative stigma of divorce to keep their husbands in an unhappy situation. These women seek to remain married in name only in order to continue to enjoy their lifestyle. They see nothing wrong with leading two completely separate lives under the same roof. They do not have to worry about paying rent, the mortgage, or other necessary expenses. They love the freedom of being able to work and have an active social life independent of their husband. They feel no obligation to cook or care for their husband. Husbands in this situation have to work very hard to obtain a divorce as well as rights to their children post-divorce. Unfortunately, this scenario can be very difficult for the whole family.

Mediation—A Better Option in Divorces

If, after trying to communicate more effectively and seeking to problem solve collaboratively, there is still no hope in the marital relationship, it is critical that the dissolution of the marriage happen in the most respectful and positive manner possible. How one manages conflict determines how satisfying the resolution of the matter will be and the effect it will have on the relationship with other person. At the heart of managing differences is speaking clearly for oneself, listening well to others, and problem solving together. This is not easy when people feel troubled, angry, or pressured. In conflicts, particularly family conflicts, a trusted, impartial third party can be helpful in directing a problem-solving process. Mediation is a dispute-resolution process in which a neutral party, the Mediator, facilitates communication between parties and assists them in reaching a mutually acceptable resolution to their dispute.

In mediation, both parties have equal participation and voice. Even where parties have attorneys, the parties themselves are given an opportunity to express their concerns without any time restraints. Mediation is far less formal than going to court. Mediators are trained in active listening and other communication skills that help the parties feel heard and understood. The mediator summarizes and reframes the issues raised by the parties in a neutral and constructive manner. This enables the parties to acknowledge the substance of the dispute from the other side's perspective, often for the very first time.

The mediation process promotes effective communication. Through the course of the mediation, parties learn how to speak and listen respectfully. This often reduces the tension and hostility accompanying the dispute. This is particularly important in cases involving family members or situations where there is a continuing relationship, such as a couple who has children, in which case the parties cannot afford to aggravate the conflict.

Disputes can be resolved far more quickly and inexpensively in mediation as compared with litigation. A mediation between parties can be scheduled and conducted within weeks, as opposed to months or even years in the litigation process. The cost of a mediation is often compared to the cost of the deposition of an expert. Mediators usually charge an hourly rate, which depends on their background, training, and level of expertise. On average, mediation fees range from $100 to $250/hour. This fee is generally shared between the parties. Mediation sessions last anywhere from two to four hours, depending on the complexity of the case. On occasion, mediations may require multiple sessions.

Mediation is confidential. Parties often desire the privacy mediation offers, particularly when the subject being discussed is personal or sensitive. In most states mediation communications are not permitted to be introduced in a later judicial or administrative proceedings, with limited exceptions.

Parties do not need an attorney to use mediation, but it is important to note that mediators, even if they are licensed attorneys, do not give legal advice in their role as mediator. Mediators can ask relevant questions to ensure parties are making informed decisions, but their role is not to advise the parties as to what is in their best interest. As a result, parties are encouraged to have independent counsel review any agreement reached in mediation prior to signing it. If parties do have lawyers, the lawyers are welcome to participate in the mediation process and provide legal guidance and support to their clients.

All case types are appropriate for mediation, but the most ideal are contested custody, visitation, child support, and property disputes. Where one or both parties want to settle but have been unable to do so on their own, a skilled mediator can assist in objectively evaluating their cases and working out a resolution. If the plaintiff's recovery is likely to be modest or the cost of litigation is significant, mediation is a better alternative. Where parties are likely to have a continuing relationship after the conclusion of the lawsuit, as in the case of divorce, mediation is a dispute-resolution process that will do as little damage as possible to the relationship. If there is extreme inequity of knowledge or bargaining power, ongoing domestic violence, or some other situation that creates an imbalance of negotiating ability, the case may be inappropriate for mediation. It is critical that mediators are mindful of these issues, as it is highly unlikely that an Indian woman will freely reveal such an imbalance of power.

Important factors for Indian families to consider when choosing a mediator include experience, reputation, educational credentials, mediation training, gender, age, cultural competency, language skills, fees, and certification by mediation organizations or courts.

Conclusion

OVER THE PAST FEW DECADES THERE HAS BEEN A SLOW but clear transformation of the Indian marriage. While India continues to have the lowest divorce rate of any country, the divorce rate among Indians is rising. Although the arranged marriage model continues to be the prevalent system of marriage among Indians, an increasing number of young Indian adults are finding their own partner on their own terms. There is no one right way for Indians to get married, and, unfortunately, there is no guarantee of success in marriage, whether it is parentally arranged or self-determined.

The family structure in America has also greatly changed over the past fifty years. Approximately half of all marriages in the United States end in divorce. A recent poll by Pew found that 44 percent of Americans under age thirty believe marriage is headed for extinction. Sociologists note that the American rate of marriage and remarriage is among the highest in the world. Half or more of the respondents in the Pew poll say that marital status is irrelevant to achieving respect, happiness, career goals, financial security, or a fulfilling sex life. However, when it comes to raising children, more than three-quarters say that it is best done when married. In 2008, 41 percent of babies were born to unmarried mothers, an eightfold increase from fifty years ago. Twenty-five percent of these children lived in a single-parent home, almost triple the number from 1960.

Conclusion

The banality of divorce tends to jade one's perspective about marriage. Immersion in Western culture can often lead to the mindset that marriages are unlikely to last forever and that if a marriage is not happy, people can always try again. Having worked with hundreds of families going through separation and divorce—Americans and Indian Americans—I find that fewer couples understand the values of love and commitment. This is not because these are difficult concepts, but because the couples have lacked a role model to demonstrate how to have a successful long-term relationship. This is one area where I feel Indian marriages have an edge, as 99 percent of Indian marriages are intact, and older-generation Indians strive to keep their marital vows.

When Indian couples are faced with a marital issue that makes continuing a relationship extremely difficult or even unsafe, they need to recognize that they have reached a point at which trying to save face is unnecessary. The most important things for both partners are safety, security, peace of mind, and good health. If these basic needs are jeopardized in a marriage and every good-faith effort has been made to address these issues to no avail, then couples must be willing to consider terminating the relationship. Mediation is the most effective non-adversarial method of resolving marital disputes.

Mediation provides an informal and efficient way for people to work out differences in a manner that serves everyone's needs and interests. The privacy of mediation enables parties to discuss sensitive matters, and the creativity that mediation encourages supports collaborative problem solving. Mediation enhances communication between parties and improves relationships, particularly where children are involved. Compliance with mediated agreements is much higher than with decisions imposed by the courts, because self-determination is a core value of mediation. When contemplating the most appropriate method by which to pursue a divorce, Indian families should seek out mediation; they can achieve a more fully satisfying resolution that will enable them to maintain a strong relationship with their children and a respectful relationship with their former partner.

Years ago, life would in essence be over for an Indian woman when she became a widow, or in the very rare instance that a couple divorced. She would be shunned by society and live in shame. She might or might not be allowed to return to her parents. Men have, on the other hand, always enjoyed the ability to remarry without any social rebuke, regardless of age. Today, Indian women and men who divorce are remarrying very successfully and leading much happier lives. A website some Indians refer to for searching for matrimonial leads is SecondShaadi.com. It seems as though individuals have learned what their needs and priorities in a relationship are after going through a bad marriage. Women are no longer stigmatized as being undesirable after divorce. Interestingly, most of the first marriages that end in divorce are arranged marriages and the successful second marriages are love marriages that are not restricted by caste, language, dowry, or other factors.

Ancient Indian scriptures understood one incredibly important point about marriage, and that is—it should be based on friendship. Prince Yudishtira in the Aranya Parva of that great epic *Mahabharata* was asked 120 questions by a Yaksha. One of the 120 questions the Yaksha asked Yudhishtira was, *"Kimsvin mitram grihesatah."* (Who is the friend of a householder?) The prince answered, *"Bhaaryaa mitram grihesatah"* (The friend of a householder is his spouse). In another question, the Yaksha asked Yudhishtira: *"Kimsvid daiva krita sakha?"* (Who is man's god-given friend?) Yudhishtira's answer was, "Bhaaryaa daivakrita sakha" (A man's God-given friend is his wife). According to Hinduism, the basis for marriage is friendship. This friendship supports the understanding, respect, and commitment that unite a man and a woman as husband and wife.

Conclusion

In most Hindu wedding ceremonies, the most important point in the ceremony is when the *Maangalya dhaaranam* occurs. This seals the bond between the bride and the groom through the tying of a golden necklace around the bride's neck by the groom. That moment is the most auspicious and sacred in the wedding, as the young man and woman become husband and wife. Immediately following the tying of the necklace, the most significant and meaningful part of the ceremony is when the couple hold hands and take seven steps together as husband and wife as they walk around Agni, the god of fire, and pledge to each other their eternal friendship. What they say after they have taken those seven steps is unquestionably the foundation for a successful marriage. Together they chant:

> *Sakhaa sapta padi bhava* *sakhyam te gameyam*
> *Sakhyam te mayoshah* *sakhyam te mayoshtah*

(With these seven steps you have become my friend. May I deserve your friendship. May my friendship make me one with you. May your friendship make you one with me.)

In order to find that special person with whom one will enjoy companionship and share life's joys, challenges, and opportunities, Indians may not have to consider horoscopes, a marriage broker, caste, dowry, or family status. However, there is still significance in identifying common values, goals, and expectations. The character traits one seeks may or may not directly relate to the Indian culture or Hindu faith, depending on one's personal predisposition to these values. I believe the success of the Indian marriage in the future is going to require self-reflection by young people regarding their needs, interests, and priorities in life, and the ability to exercise good judgment and effective interpersonal skills to identify a compatible partner. Anticipating potential areas of disagreement and clarifying expectations in advance of committing to a long-term marital relationship is critical. Once the couple has married, clear and effective communication, respect, trust, and collaborative problem solving can address most issues that arise, ensuring a long and fulfilling marital relationship.

As poet and Noble Prize winner Rabindranath Tagore said, "Only in Love are unity and duality not in conflict."

References

Diwan, Paras. *Family Law: Law of Marriage and Divorce in India.* New Delhi: Sterling Publishers Private Limited, 1983.

Fisher, Roger, and William Ury. *Getting to Yes: Negotiating Agreement Without Giving In.* Penguin Books, 1991.

Luscombe, Belinda. "Who Needs Marriage?" *Time Magazine,* November 29, 2010.

Pandya, Meenal Atul. *Vivah: Design a Perfect Hindu Wedding.* MeeRa Publications, January 10, 2000.

Rao, V. V. Prakasa. *Marriage, the Family and Women in India.* Printox: South Asia Books, 1982.

Thomas, Kenneth W., and Ralph H. Kilman. *Thomas-Kilman Conflict Mode Instrument.* CPP Inc., 2007.

About the Author

G EETHA RAVINDRA IS an attorney, mediator, and trainer with over twenty years of experience in the field of Alternative Dispute Resolution. She is currently the mediator for the International Monetary Fund. Geetha served as director of the Department of Dispute Resolution Services at the Supreme Court of Virginia from 1996–2007 and managed the Dalkon Shield Arbitration Program at the Private Adjudication Center from 1992–1996. She has been an adjunct professor at the University of Richmond School of Law and the College of William and Mary Law School teaching mediation. Geetha is a short term consultant with the World Bank and provides both mediation services and conflict resolution training.

Geetha has mediated family cases for the Richmond City Juvenile and Domestic Relations District Court for over fifteen years. She also provides assistance to Indian families dealing with difficult marital issues. Geetha has mediated workplace matters for the U.S. Navy, Veterans Administration, Department of Energy, and Virginia Employment Dispute Resolution Agency. She provides communication and conflict resolution training for NASA and several Virginia agencies, including the Workers Compensation Commission, Department of Health, Virginia Employment Commission, and the Department of Justice Services. Geetha facilitates management retreats for several organizations, including the World Bank and Washington D.C. Department of Health.

Geetha is vice chair of the Dispute Resolution Section of the American Bar Association, chair of the Joint ADR Committee (which is a joint committee of the Virginia Bar Association and Virginia State Bar), past president of Virginia Mediation Network, and the past chair of the Virginia State Bar Attorney Client Fee Dispute Resolution Program. She has several published articles on court-connected dispute resolution. She also conducts training programs and presentations related to alternative dispute resolution around the country and has provided mediation training in India, where she assisted in the development of a court-connected mediation program for the High Court of Madras.

Geetha Ravindra was born in Mysore, India and moved to the United States in 1970. She is married to Dr. P. V. Ravindra and has two children, Lakshmi and Krishna. She is a member of the Board of the Hindu Center of Virginia and teaches a religious studies course to high school students at the Richmond Temple. Geetha can be reached at info@shaadiremix.com. For more information please visit Shaadiremix.com.